I0474703

Chambersburg, PA 17202
http://simplelocalbusiness.com

Courtney Engle Robertson works as a digital media strategist with a focus on small business owners. She develops the blueprints and architecture for businesses online presence, launches and optimizes their presentation, and trains owners to operate and implement strategy for building beyond the basics.

As a former business educator, Courtney's strength is in helping others learn and be able to implement actions that will help them succeed. As she transitioned from the public school classrooms to business owners offices, she has focused on streamlining the efforts needed to grow their customer base using social media, local search engine optimization, websites built in WordPress, and mobile marketing.

To my husband Matthew, who has created a space for me to shine while always making me laugh.

To my family, who have stuck by me through all the ups and downs.

To my Heavenly Father, who's love never fails.

If you'd like to receive updates to this book as LinkedIn changes or additional bonus content, please sign up at http://simplelocalbusiness.com/books/linkedin/updates/.

If this book has helped you get started or further understand LinkedIn, please leave a review at http://simplelocalbusiness.com/books/linkedin/review-linkedin-local-small-business/

Are you ready to expand your business or career online? My goal is to help you and your business shine online with a practical guide to get you there. This book will guide you through maximizing your network within LinkedIn. Take your time building your profile and walking through these steps.

Consider this more of a manual loaded with images rather than a topical book about LinkedIn. As such, don't race ahead but rather do the work as you go through the book.

Changes can and will happen to LinkedIn and other online tools. It is my goal to update the content of this book as these changes occur. Please sign up to be notified about further updates.

I look forward to hearing how this book impact's your presence. At the end of the book, you'll find a way to get further updates as LinkedIn will always be updating features.

LINKEDIN OVERVIEW

Ask most people that have a LinkedIn account how they use it and the majority will likely indicate that they set it up when job hunting as an online resume.   Few will say they found job postings that way, and far fewer will say they have found value in business networking. These opinions are common but LinkedIn's value is becoming more clear each day. Though LinkedIn launched <u>May 5, 2003</u>, it is still gaining momentum for continuing business networking relationships offline.

While Twitter can build a network and continue the ongoing conversation, and Facebook can be a blur between professional and private life, LinkedIn is expected to be business to business networking. LinkedIn's focus is entirely upon your professional life. When you meet others at networking events, you can extend that connection using LinkedIn for online networking. Rather than just swapping business cards, use that opportunity to digitally swap cards with LinkedIn's CardMunch mobile app, or look up new connection on LinkedIn and request a connection.

What about you? What goals do you have for your career or business? Do you know how LinkedIn can help you reach those goals? When you establish your purpose, LinkedIn can be incredibly powerful to help you reach those goals.

Think of LinkedIn as an incredibly large networking event. You'll need to determine who to focus your attention on, which people to approach, and how to connect with them in a meaningful way that isn't overly self-promotional. You want to truly build a relationship with other networkers that benefits them as well as yourself.

You are on LinkedIn as a way to cultivate a network of referrals. As my friend and mentor <u>Bob Burg</u> says "All things being equal, people do business with, and refer business to, people they know, like, and trust." In his book, <u>Endless Referrals</u>, Bob shares practical yet profound insights into strategies for building a business with referrals, as well as in the parable series "The Go-Giver". I highly recommend these books as foundational networking training. Buy building your referral network, online or off, you are in the business of helping people reach their goals, which is more than just a nice way to do business, it is a successful and profitable way. Incorporating this into your approach to LinkedIn will make all the difference in the results you reach.   1

Getting Familiar

It's important to get familiar with LinkedIn's layout and key terms as you navigate your way through networking. During the login process you will complete most of your profile, but we'll revisit that later to tweak it.

Your dashboard in LinkedIn is your source of updates and inspiration. You'll see what your connections are updating, whether as a status update, or just general activity within LinkedIn, suggested connections, and a review of who is viewing your profile.

The top navigation toolbar is your easiest way to get around in LinkedIn. You can specify what category you'd like to search:

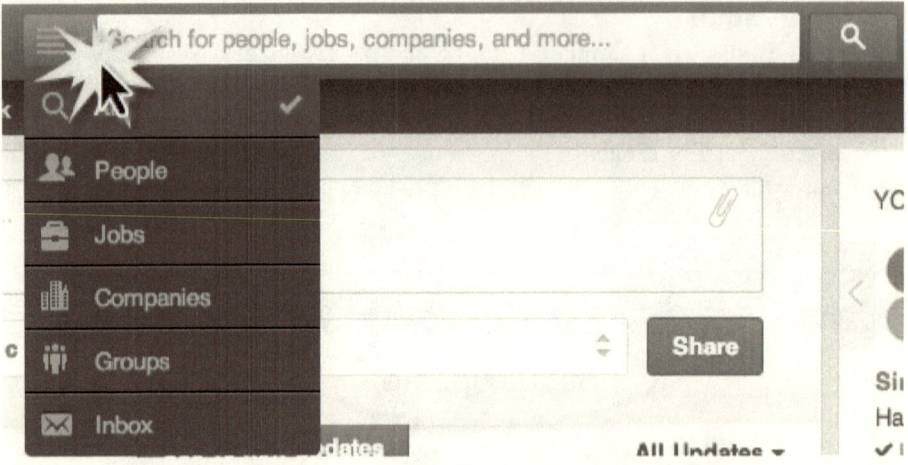

You can see a preview of your inbox messages. Your requests to connect will show up here, so check it often:

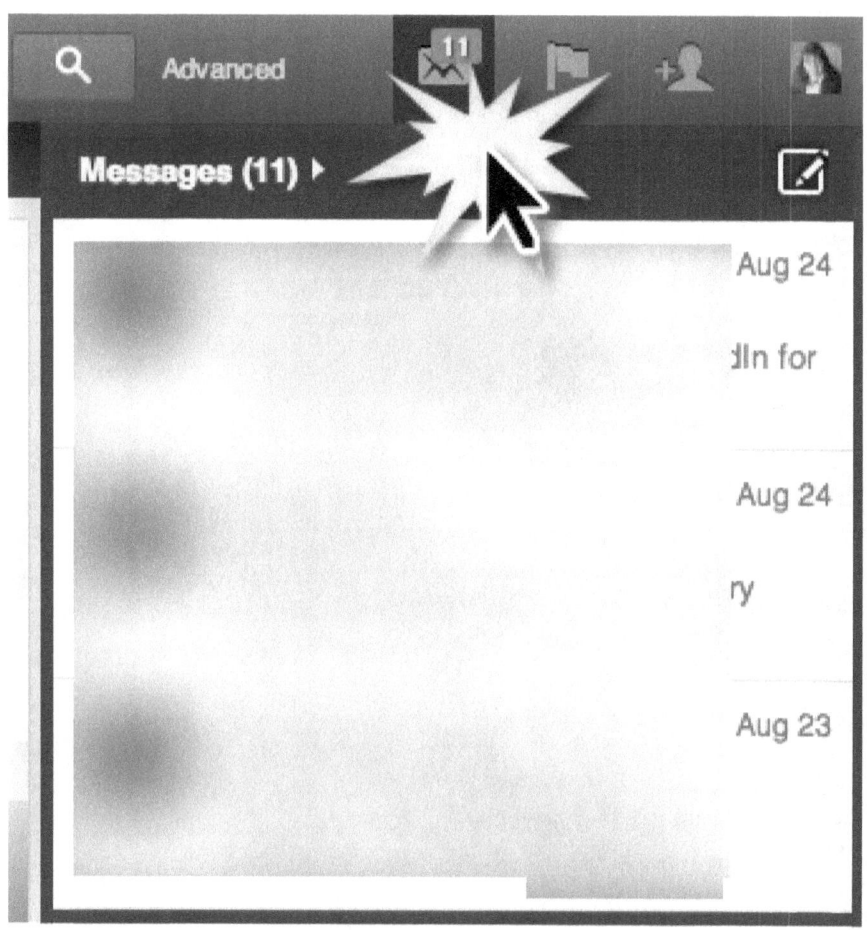

Alerts tell you about any replies or other notifications that you've received:

Courtney Robertson

Q   Advanced   +11

Notifications ▸

35 people commented on a discussion   2h
that you followed in Social Media News,

endorsed you for a skill: 12h
Marketing

Change Management, Organiza...   17h
is now a connection

8 people also congratulated   19h
on the new job, Chief Digital Strategist at
Bell Digital Strategies

endorsed you for 3 skills: 1d
Marketing, Blogging, Online
Marketing

See the quick shortcut to add contacts:

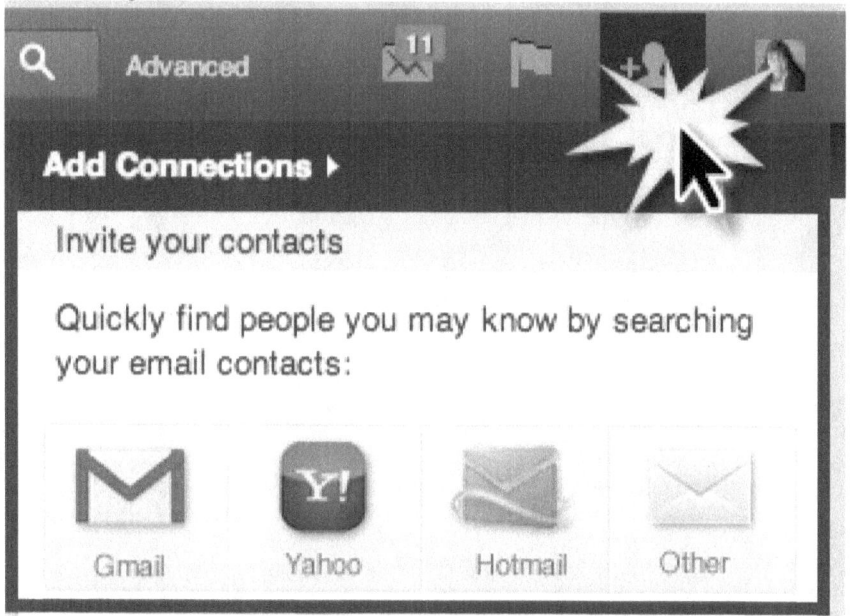

Your profile icon serves as a shortcut to your account settings:

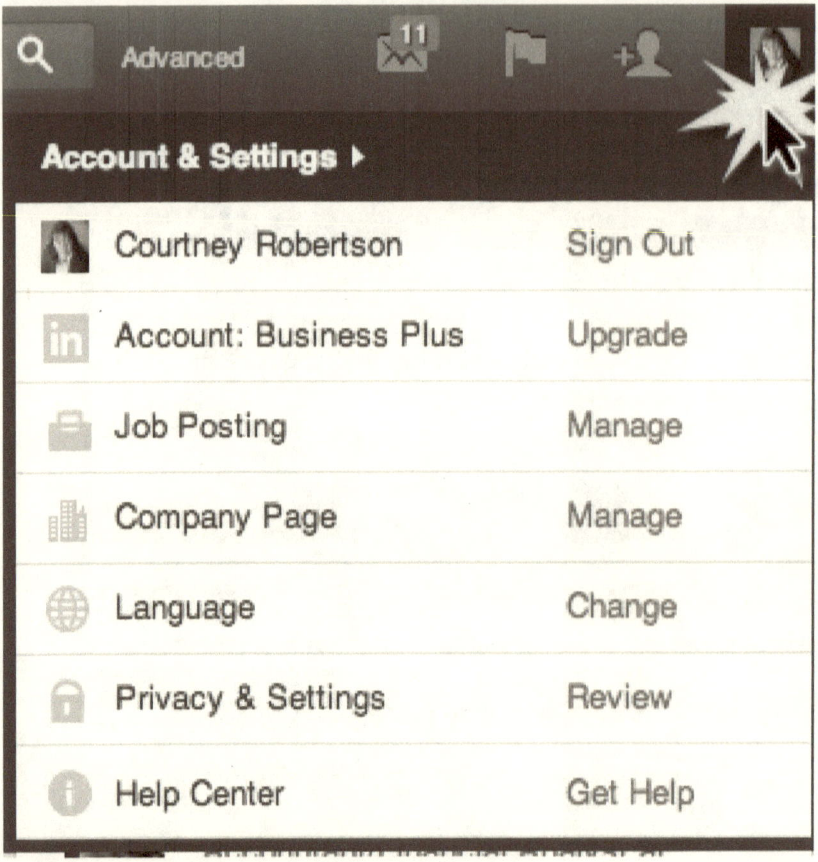

Q Advanced   11   🚩   +👤   👤

Account & Settings ▶

👤 Courtney Robertson	Sign Out
in Account: Business Plus	Upgrade
💼 Job Posting	Manage
🏢 Company Page	Manage
🌐 Language	Change
🔒 Privacy & Settings	Review
ⓘ Help Center	Get Help

And finally, if you are a paying member, see the business tools menu:

Business Tools   Upgrade

Post a Job

Talent Solutions

Advertise

We'll take a look more closely at the rest of the layouts within each section of LinkedIn as we go, but you now have the basics to get around.

Go Slow to Grow

While I'd like to think this book is all you need to have a fantastic experience with LinkedIn, it really isn't. The truth is, what you need to have that experience is experience. You need to really slow down and grab every little tip, check every possible setting, and complete every part of your account. You need to build in an ongoing manner and actively interact on LinkedIn.

This book is designed to be sure you are thorough in your approach, provoke you to consider a few perspectives, and help you clearly accomplish your goals. Reading this book isn't enough. You need to do the work of building your network like your business and paycheck depend upon it.

Planning Your Strategy:

Knowing what your intentions are with LinkedIn will help guide what activity and connections that you build with your profile. Consider the following goals and weigh the importance each has for you and your company:

1. Boost website traffic
2. Increase your network connections
3. Increase personal and company brand exposure
4. Increase email list subscribers
5. Increase conference and webinar attendees
6. Grow your LinkedIn group
7. PR and media opportunities
8. Speaking opportunities
9. Leads
10. Sales

Dive In!

With your mind set on what you want from your experience, it's time to get started building your profile. Ready?

UNDERSTANDING HOW TO GET FOUND

Before we even get started building your LinkedIn profile, it is important to know what you can do to help people discover you. To do that, you need to think like the ideal person that will find you via LinkedIn's search.

Keywords

Let's say I'm hunting for a tax accountant. I may turn to LinkedIn to find a professional in my network that specializes in these services. By searching for "tax accountant", I can find a variety of providers. You'll see that the phrases I used in my search are highlighted. Take note where in the users profile preview that you can see these keywords. These are the places where keywords matter most.

Likewise, view someone's complete profile that turns up in that search result and see where the keywords are also used throughout the whole profile.

Summary

I've spent most of my working years at Keller Financial Group where we strive to help our clients and their families protect, preserve and grow their wealth. With integrity and honesty, we will help individuals and businesses plan and prepare for a secure future through sound financial analysis and by providing products and services that help them achieve their goals.

Specialties: taxes, accounting, protecting financial assets, financial planning, investment services, retirement planning, estate planning, comprehensive financial plan & analysis, debt management strategies, tax reduction strategies, succession planning, business transition planning, college planning, individual income tax preparation, LLC/Partnership/Corporations income tax preparation, business accounting & compilation, web-based accounting

 Experience

President, CPA
Keller Financial Group

January 1987 – Present (26 years 8 months) | Carlisle, Mechanicsburg, and Central Pennsylvania

Services include:

Tax Services for individuals and businesses
Accounting Services
Business Advisory
Financial Planning
Investment Services
Estate Planning
Retirement Solutions

We provide solutions to enable our clients to achieve their goals. Our tax, accounting, financial planning, and investment professionals will be faithful stewards in all that is entrusted to our care. We will have a positive influence on all with whom we come in contact.

Dwayne Keller is a Registered Representative of INVEST Financial Corporation, member FINRA (www.finra.org) (www.SIPC.org) INVEST and its affiliated insurance agencies offer securities, advisory services, and certain insurance products and are not affiliated with Keller Financial Group, Inc. Products offered are –Not insured by the FDIC/NCUA – not a deposit or other obligation of or guaranteed by any bank/credit union – subject to risks including the possible loss of principal amount invested.

INVEST Privacy Policy (http://www.investfinancial.com/public/forms/ifc_madv6130a.pdf). Content posted by other parties does not necessarily represent the views of INVEST, Keller Financial Group Inc. or Dwayne Keller. Content is for general purposes only and is not an offer to buy or sell any security. INVEST does not provide tax or legal advice.

Knowing what keywords to use is equally as important as knowing where to focus those keywords for optimal search results. We'll look further at these sections while we complete your profile, but the top areas to focus on will be:

1.   Your headline
2.   Your summary (and specialties)
3.   Skills & expertise
4.   Your interests

Think Like Your Potential Clients

What words would people needing your service search for? You may be a freelance concierge for hire, but I might search for laundry service or bike messenger. Write a list of all the terms that others might use when seeking what you have to offer. Remember, think as though you're the client. Use simple terms or even specific areas of service that you offer. Then ask a friend to describe what you do. Write down any other terms they use. Finally, search the web for your competition and read what they are saying on their websites and social profiles. Once you have this list of ideas, be sure to use them when we get to building your profile.

Watch those endings

If I search for accountant or accounting, I should still et the same results in theory. However, most search engines don't yet accommodate for those options. Use variations of your job title that use these endings:

*   ed
*   ing
*   s

Positioning Your Profile for Value

If you were to describe what you do to someone else, do you say just your job title and assume they understand what value that has for them? What if you could share the value of your profession, giving others a clear idea about how working with you will benefit their business? People care more about "*What's in it for me?*". Always consider that while your job title may be "tax accountant", I might be searching for "payroll". Rather than just sticking to "tax accountant at XYZ Inc." your headline might do better to read: "Saving hours effort in payroll processing while providing tax accountant services".

YOUR PROFILE

Your personal profile on LinkedIn is the place to showcase your expertise and talents. It is your professional presence as a walking ambassador of your company. However, it is not and should not be confused with your brand or company presence; this is reserved for LinkedIn Company Pages.

By maintaining your profile and building your network beyond job-hunting, you'll have an established community long before you need to call in any favors. Better still, you will be helping connect others and clearly identify what type of support or referrals you might like.

While your profile may look similar to a résumé, it is not entirely the same. It may still be helpful that you have a traditional résumé available in other means, or even to use your LinkedIn profile to jump-start your résumé.

Your profile consists of the following parts:
- Name & headline
- Activity
- Background
  - Summary
  - Multimedia
- Experience
- Organizations
- Certifications
- Courses
- Skills & Expertise
- Education
- Additional Information
  - Interests
  - Personal Details
  - Advice for Contacting
- Recommendations
  - Received
  - Given
- Connections

- Groups
- Following
  - News
  - Companies
- People You May Know (PYMK)
- Optional
  - Test Scores
  - Courses
  - Patents
  - Certifications
  - Volunteering & Causes
  - Projects
  - Languages
  - Publications
  - Honors & Awards

Getting Started:

As you begin the process of building your profile, it will be handy to have a recent copy of a résumé on file, along with a recent professional quality photo (well lit, and better than webcam quality). LinkedIn will update you on how complete your profile is as you walk through the initial profile setup. The levels of completeness are:

- Just beginning
- Intermediate
- Advanced
- Expert
- All star

Name and Headline:

When completing your profile, enter your common name. If your proper name is Charles, but you go by and are known by Chuck or even your middle name instead, complete the profile using the name people will recognize you by. You can enter an alias name, such as your formal or proper first name, a maiden name, or any other name changes that may help people find you.

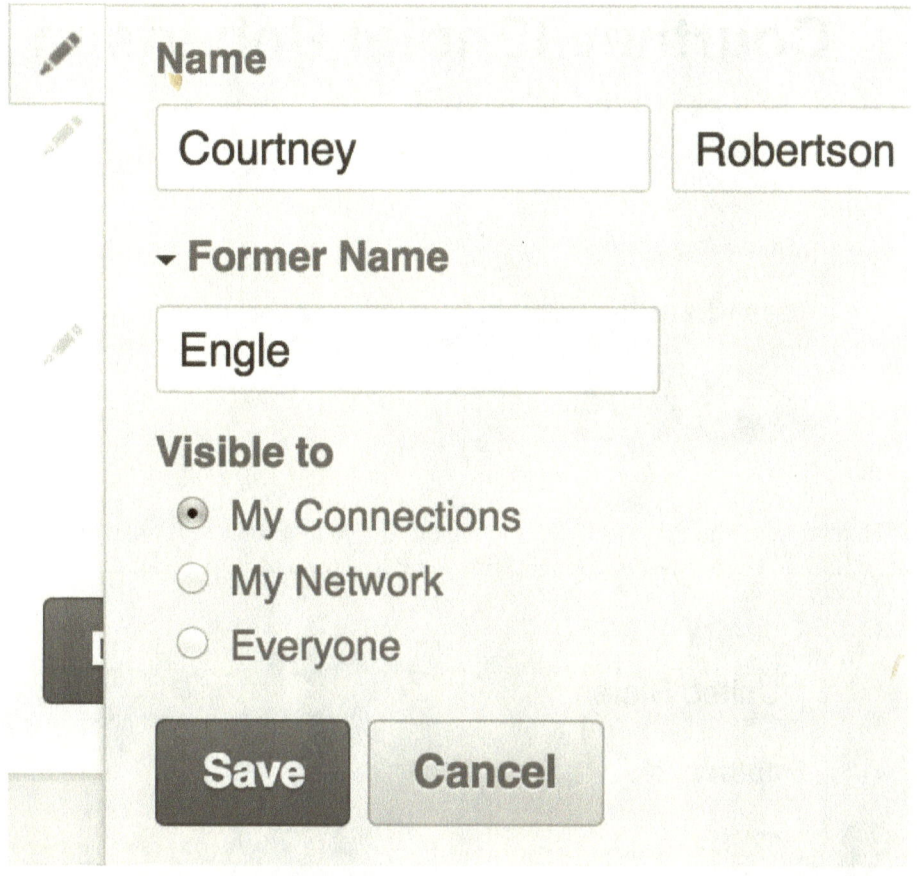

Your headline is a unique area to stand out. By default, it will display your most recent job position. However, it will help you stand out when later you participate in groups, company pages, or replying to others updates. This is a chance to fill out your mission statement concisely, and is keyword rich, though limited to a mere 120 characters. I have included my headline as:

◎ Helping ⇒ Small Business Owners ⇐ by Streamlining Social Media, Mobile Marketing, WordPress & Local SEO ◎

By doing so, the custom characters help my headline pop when compared to others also listed, and the core of my intentions for connecting on LinkedIn are shared. These headlines are visible elsewhere in LinkedIn, like viewing a list of all members in a group.

Courtnev (Enale) Robertson

Your professional headline

◎ Helping ⇒ Small Business Owners ⇐ by Strea

Show examples

See what other users in your industry are using ▸

[Save] [Cancel]

Finally, you should specify your region in your profile. People in your neighborhood may want to connect with you based around your region.

Country

United States ▲▼

Postal code

17201

Location name

⦿ **Chambersburg, Pennsylvania**

○ **Harrisburg, Pennsylvania Area**

Industry

Professional Training & Coaching ▲▼

[Save] [Cancel]

Activity

Activity can be any links that you share, status updates, or any other activity on

LinkedIn that you allow to be public.

To see the statistics of who has viewed your status updates, on the main LinkedIn page, view the column on the right side. Look for "Who's Viewed Your Updates":

This will help you determine the interaction and reach of your updates. By learning what your connections engage with and at what times will help you improve the reach of each update. With greater reach, you will stay "front of mind" with your connections. I'd recommend at least one status update per day, and you can test to measure further from there.

Summary

Your Summary is the where you will shine the most. While people can review your previous employment, what they really want to know is what's in it for them? What is your intention for your presence in LinkedIn?

While LinkedIn doesn't do much to help you format your summary in unique ways, you'll still have the chance to use 2,000 characters to shine. You can use all capital letters as headings, empty spaces to create sections, and unique characters as bullet points.

It is important to use keywords that your ideal prospects will use to find you. Think like them. What words will they search for? What will help them read your profile quickly and have a lasting impression?

I've divided my profile into a few sections:

- Overview (the initial keyword dense description of what products or

services you offer)
- o   Include your location
- o   Personal mission statement
- Personal description of experiences and expertise you excel in
- Areas of focus - more descriptive version of products/services
- What's in it for them or why are you on LinkedIn?
- Specialties - an additional 500 characters to share unique areas of focus or highlight briefly areas that aren't overtly related to your core business

Notice how quickly your eye can scan a summary:

Multimedia

Those that have an existing profile will notice that the "Applications" area of your profile has vanished and in its place is the new multimedia widget. This is a place to showcase your portfolio, to include a video describing what your strengths are, and share presentations of a wide variety.

You can showcase at least 5 unique multimedia options in your profile. At this time, the items are in the order that you load them. The only way to shuffle items is to delete what you want removed until the preferred item is first. More than 5 items are viewable, but hidden below a "see more" link.

Go to the Edit mode, and at the bottom of your summary section, you can add rich media content easily by adding a link to the specific content. See the list of supported audio, video, photo, presentation, and other content platforms supported.

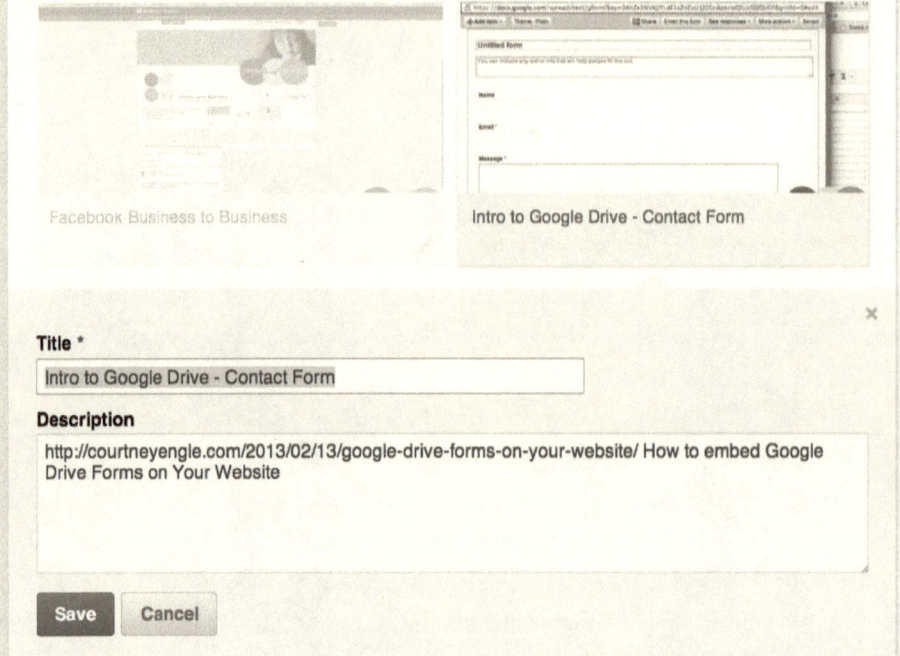

Experience

The area most like a resume within your LinkedIn profile is the Experience section. You have up to 100 characters to use in the Position Title of your profile, and these are keyword sensitive. Word the job title based upon how others would search to discover you, not based upon what payroll referred to your position as.

Likewise, you have 2,000 characters to describe what you did at each position you've held. Expand upon your descriptions and like the Summary Background section, use special characters and capitalization to format this section for easy readability. Be sure to include skills that can apply to future positions and opportunities that you are interested in. Within the career development world, the idea of transferrable skills shows your willingness to apply existing skills for what the future holds.

Avoid updating your headline with each position you list. Using your headline as a brief introduction is more compelling than a job title for a headline.

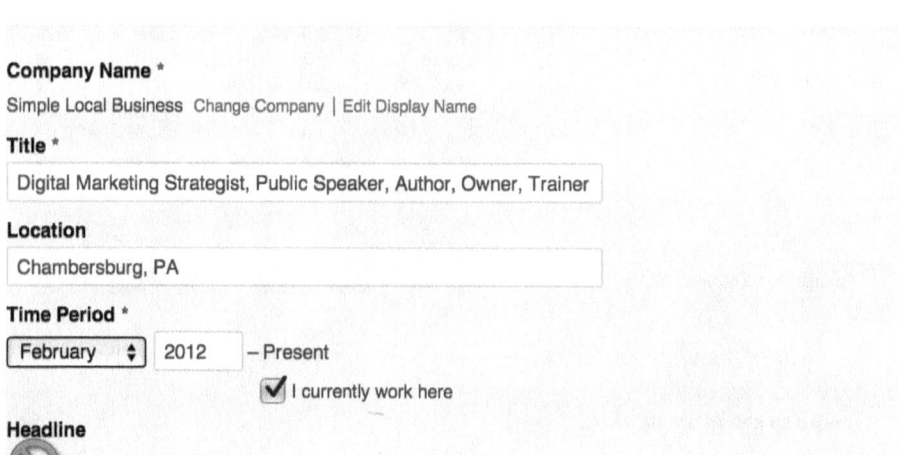

EXPERIENCE ✦ Add | ⋮

Company Name *

Simple Local Business Change Company | Edit Display Name

Title *

Digital Marketing Strategist, Public Speaker, Author, Owner, Trainer

Location

Chambersburg, PA

Time Period *

February ⬍   2012   – Present

☑ I currently work here

Headline

🚫 Update my headline to:

Description

Helping small business owners streamline social media, local SEO, and marketing by providing support and training

Skills & Endorsements

You can <u>include</u> up to 50 different skills and areas of expertise on your profile that have a maximum of 61 characters. These skills are not as stringent as a recommendation. As people visit your profile, they will be asked to endorse these skills with just one click to approve, rather than a lengthy written recommendation. When you visit LinkedIn's skills page, you will see a list of corresponding skills that others have included as well.

By initially keeping the minimal approach to skills, you can focus what people will endorse. As you gain endorsements for various skills, consider expanding your skills to maximize the search results.

SKILLS & EXPERTISE ✎ | ↕

Most endorsed for...

99+	Social Media Marketing
57	Online Marketing
38	Blogging
28	SEO
25	Social Media
24	Facebook
22	Wordpress
19	Mobile Marketing
17	Social Media Measurement

Skills will be listed in order of those with the most endorsements. Additional skills are still viewable.

Courtney also knows about...

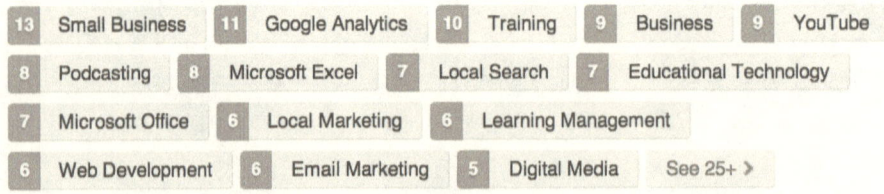

13 Small Business	11 Google Analytics	10 Training	9 Business	9 YouTube
8 Podcasting	8 Microsoft Excel	7 Local Search	7 Educational Technology	
7 Microsoft Office	6 Local Marketing	6 Learning Management		
6 Web Development	6 Email Marketing	5 Digital Media	See 25+ >	

Education

Educational background information can help share your qualifications for a new position, but should not be limited to just that. Additional connections may occur because you share the same alma mater. By describing your educational background, you are opening your profile further for more search results. Be as thorough as possible here.

 **EDUCATION**

Shippensburg University of Pennsylvania ✎ ⊡ ↕
Masters, Masters of Business Administration
2002 – 2002

⊡ **Add your videos, images, documents...**

Bloomsburg University of Pennsylvania ✎ ⊡ ↕
BS, Business, Computer, and Information Techonology

To further complete your profile, you can include a variety of other experience as well. Remember that each additional section of optional information that you provide is still keyword rich. By further completing these sections, you have that many more chances at being discovered in search results and featuring your best work.

- Courses
- Certifications
- Organizations
- Honors & Awards
- Volunteering
- Test Scores

 COURSES ✎

Bloomsburg University of Pennsylvania

- Student Teaching - Cumberland Perry Area Vocational Technical School - BCIT Field Experience
- Intro to Programming
- Networking
- Business Information Systems
- Psychology of Education
- Intro the Exceptional Individual - Gifted & Special Education
- Accounting I & II
- Business Communication

 # CERTIFICATIONS

Water Safety Instructor
American Red Cross
September 2003 – September 2007

Lifeguard, First Aid, CPR, AED
American Red Cross
December 1999 – September 2007

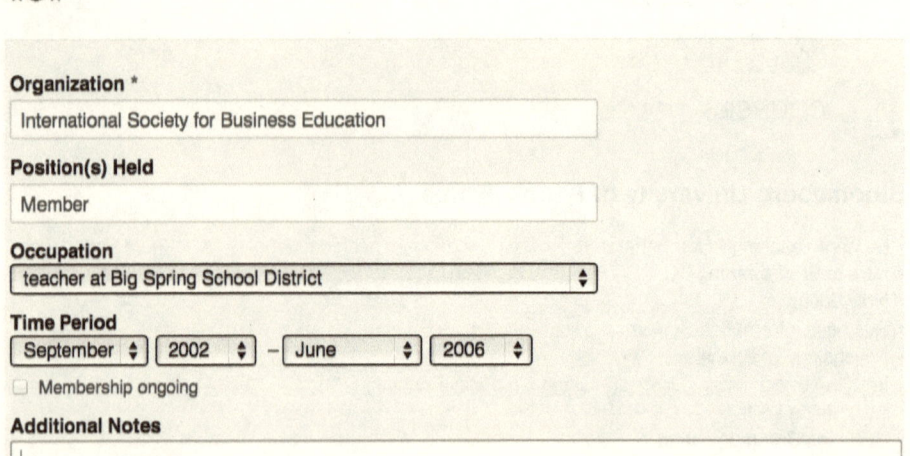

ORGANIZATIONS   ✦ Add ⇳

Organization *

International Society for Business Education

Position(s) Held

Member

Occupation

teacher at Big Spring School District

Time Period

September ⇕ | 2002 ⇕ | – | June ⇕ | 2006 ⇕

☐ Membership ongoing

Additional Notes

|

Recommendations

LinkedIn <u>Recommendations</u> are a more formal approach to endorsements and have been a part of a LinkedIn profile since the beginning. Recommendations are really a way to show potential clients, employers, and strategic partners your reputation with others. There is some indication that increased recommendations lead to higher search ranking, so it is important to seek recommendations. If you manage to get 10+ recommendations, you can join the Top Recommended People group or if you have 25 - 99 recommendations you can join the subgroup Top Recommended People Gold, 100 - 175 Platinum, or even 175 - 500 Diamond.

Writing a Recommendation:

When you write a recommendation for others, there are a few key points to remember.

1. Add value to the other person's profile by staying on topic.
2. Type your recommendation into a word processing program to proofread for spelling and grammar.
3. Mention specific skills and strengths the person has to offer based upon the skills and objectives the person has mentioned on his or her personal profile.
   - If this is a business owner, focus on what makes them unique or the best at what they do.
   - If this is a colleague, focus on transferrable skills that they can use in further employment opportunities.
   - Observe this person's personal brand in the profile and adjust your recommendation accordingly.
4. Share how you know this person. LinkedIn now allows you to endorse people for specific jobs they've held, but still share what your professional role was with him or her.
5. Be brief in your description with a maximum of 100 words. People want to know if this is someone to conduct business with, not read their life summary as told by you. Consider using descriptive adjectives that really set your recommendation apart from others.

To write a recommendation, go to the person's profile that you'd like to write a review about or go to Profile —> Recommendations —> Given. You can see a list of other recommendations you've made here but at the bottom you can begin creating a new recommendation.

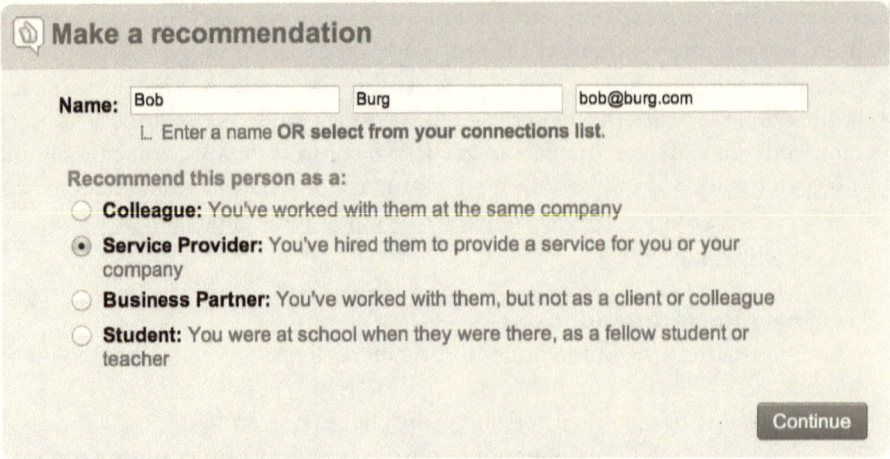

You will need to select which of the positions this person has listed that you would like to recommend. Be sure to read that part of their profile closely before submitting your recommendation.

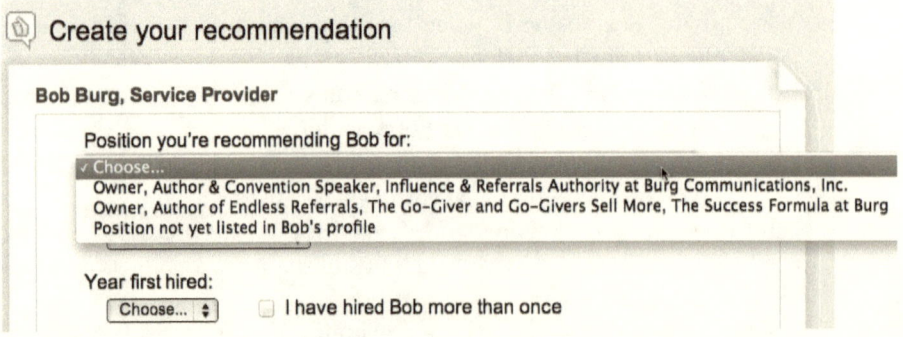

Next, LinkedIn asks you which attributes this person possesses. This is a newer feature to recommendations, but do share what makes this person great to connect with.

Top Attributes

Choose **THREE attributes** that best describe this service provider:

- ☐ **Great Results:** Superlative work, from concept to final output
- ☐ **Personable:** Works well with colleagues and clients
- ☑ **Expert:** Deep and detailed knowledge of the subject
- ☑ **Good Value:** Excellent work at a reasonable cost
- ☐ **On Time:** Punctual at each step of the process
- ☑ **High Integrity:** Trustworthy, consistent, and reliable
- ☐ **Creative:** Inventive, out-of-the-box ideas and implementation

Finally, place your well-crafted recommendation into the form box and submit.

Written Recommendation

Write a brief recommendation for Bob. Recommendations you write will appear on your profile.

Example: Bob is a detail-oriented manager who watches the balance sheet like a hawk without losing sight of the strategic objective.

A message will be sent to Bob with your recommendation. [view / edit]

Send or Cancel

You can write recommendations for others as part of a strategy to garner recommendations yourself, or even overtly ask to swap recommendations. Be cautious with this swap approach. Your recommendations should always be genuine. It is a good gesture to write recommendations for others that have stood out to you, whether in services provided, coworkers, or peers in the same industry.

Viewing Recommendations Received:

Like writing a recommendation, you can see recommendations you've received by either viewing them on your own profile or by going to Profile —> Recommendations. Each time that you receive a recommendation, you'll receive an inbox notification in LinkedIn, allowing you to authorize publishing that recommendation before it goes live for others to view or even to request a modification.

You have **3 recommendations** (3 visible) for this position. To show or hide recommendations, select them and click Save Changes.

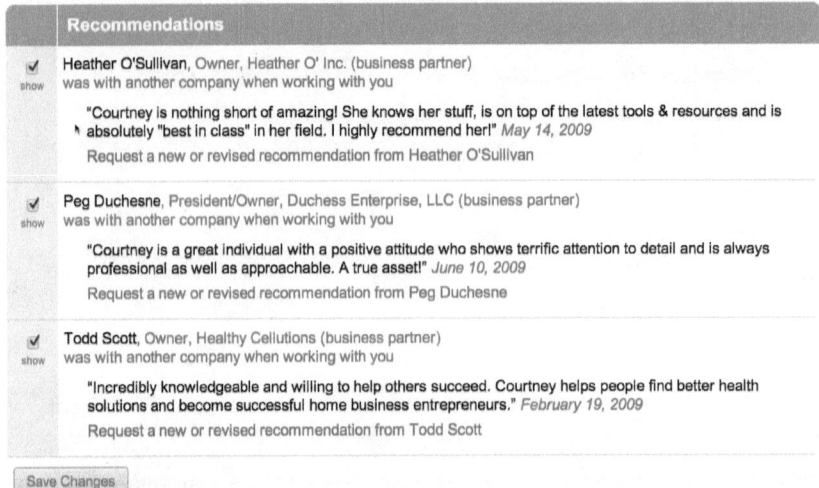

Recommendations

☑ **Heather O'Sullivan**, Owner, Heather O' Inc. (business partner)
show was with another company when working with you
 	
    "Courtney is nothing short of amazing! She knows her stuff, is on top of the latest tools & resources and is absolutely "best in class" in her field. I highly recommend her!" *May 14, 2009*
    Request a new or revised recommendation from Heather O'Sullivan

☑ **Peg Duchesne**, President/Owner, Duchess Enterprise, LLC (business partner)
show was with another company when working with you
 	
    "Courtney is a great individual with a positive attitude who shows terrific attention to detail and is always professional as well as approachable. A true asset!" *June 10, 2009*
    Request a new or revised recommendation from Peg Duchesne

☑ **Todd Scott**, Owner, Healthy Cellutions (business partner)
show was with another company when working with you
 	
    "Incredibly knowledgeable and willing to help others succeed. Courtney helps people find better health solutions and become successful home business entrepreneurs." *February 19, 2009*
    Request a new or revised recommendation from Todd Scott

Save Changes

Requesting Recommendations:

Asking others to provide you a recommendation is important, and you should still set a goal for getting multiple recommendations for the key positions you've listed on your profile. Do remember that you are asking others for their time and thought into writing a recommendation. Customize each request that you send, and don't use LinkedIn's default message. Prewriting the recommendation or at least listing key bullet points for that person can keep their recommendation relevant and refresh their memory.

Start by sending requests one at a time. You should personalize each message and include the person's name in the body of your request. If you send in bulk, you might ask 200 people the same "Dear Jon" introduction.

To ask for recommendations, view your profile, select the drop-down menu from "Edit Profile", or visit this link: http://www.linkedin.com/recRequests?cor=&trk=prof-0-sb-ask_for_rec-link.

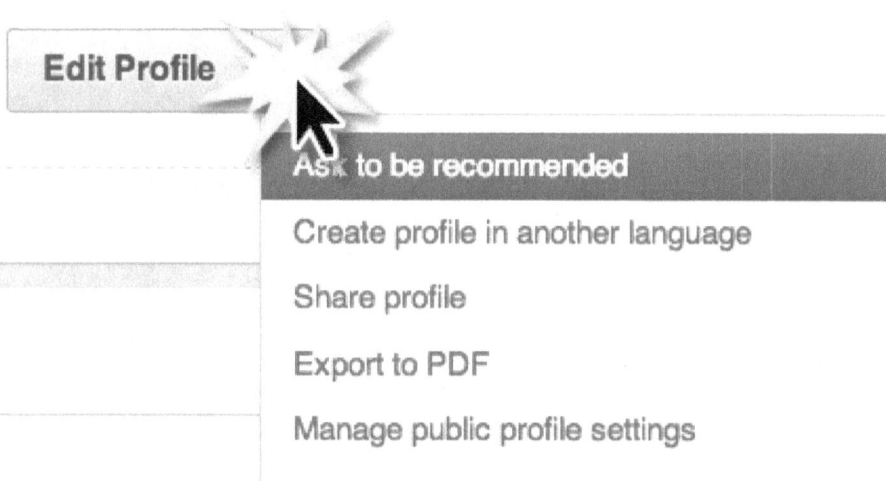

Then send your pre-written request. Remember to spell and grammar check this.

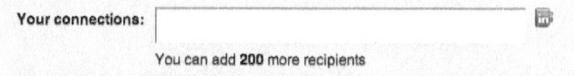

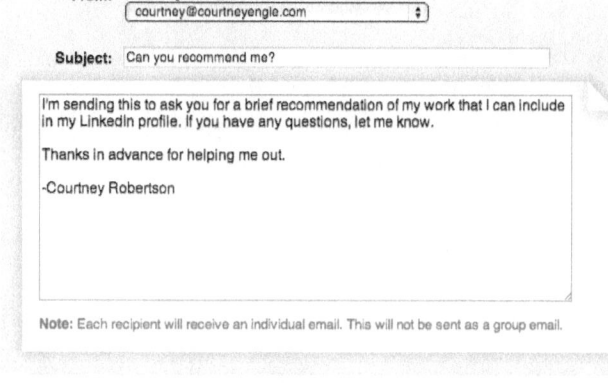

Remember to thank the person for their review and consider writing a recommendation for them as well, whether they've requested it or not. If they don't want it published, they can decide on that.

Additional Information

Interests are an additional way to make use of those keywords. They really can be anything on or off topic, so long as it isn't entirely unprofessional.

Your Personal Details are entirely your choice to display or not.

Advice for Contacting You is again a great keyword place, as well as a place to list a business phone, email, or even a link (though it won't be a clickable link). I use this area as a way for people to find my email address, in the event that they have reached their capacity to invite connections without knowing their email addresses. I highly recommend doing this, but using a Gmail or other webmail provider rather than your main email inbox.

 ADDITIONAL INFO

Interests

social media, education, personal development, wellness, health, nutrition, relationship marketing, personal branding, violin, mandolin, swimming, concerts, coffee

Personal Details

Birthday   May 12, 1979
Marital Status   Married

Advice for Contacting Courtney

Connect with me here (courane01+Li@gmail.com) and online anywhere else: http://courtneyengle.com/contact

Connections

Your connections can be viewed by others or you can disable that setting. Since I tend to be a more open networker, I allow my connections to be seen by others. The choice really is yours.

Keith Johnson
America's #1 Confidence Coach ▲ | ...

Don Nori Sr.
Founder, Destiny Image; Author; Speak...

Dave Saunders
Product Management, Product Marketin...

Viveka von Rosen
Author of Wiley's "LinkedIn Marketing: H...

Bob Burg
Bestselling Author & Convention Speak...

Thom Scott
Vice President of Marketing, Chief Instig...

Groups

We will dive deep into LinkedIn groups in other chapters. However, as groups relate to your profile, you should know that groups that you join can be visible or hidden from those viewing your profile.

GROUPS

Bloomsburg Universi...
Visible ▸

BrandYou
Visible ▸

Central Penn Busine...
Visible ▸

Christian Profession...
Visible ▸

Digital Marketing
Visible ▸

Entrepreneurs in Soc...
Visible ▸

Google APPS users
Visible ▸

See 43 more ▸

Following

When others view your profile, they can see the news and companies you are following. Unlike groups, you cannot hide what you are following from others. We will address News and Company in future sections.

Who's Viewed Your Profile

Depending upon your account settings and membership level, you can see who has viewed your account. For this, you will need to switch from Edit Profile to Profile -> View Profile and look on the right column.

WHO'S VIEWED YOUR PROFILE

5 Your profile has been viewed by 5 people in the past 3 days.

39 You have shown up in search results 39 times in the past 3 days.

When you click on the blue text displaying who viewed your profile, you have a few options. If you want the ability to look at other people's profiles without their knowledge, keep your settings private. Select profile view settings to preview how others that have viewing profiles enabled will see.

If I am viewing other people's profiles and do not want them to know, I'll keep it anonymous for a short period of time. However, I do want to know who's viewed my profile and most of the time am willing for others to discover that I've viewed their profile. I usually let the profile viewing settings open and occasionally switch briefly.

Profile Stats

See Who's Viewed Your Profile

Get a brand new perspective with more real names, profile views and search insights

How you will appear

Courtney Robert
© Helping ⇒ Small Busi
Local SEO ©

Your profile view must be changed to see profile stats:
- from Invisible: characteristics (eg. industry and title)
- to Visible: Your name and headline (why?)

You can change this setting back at any time.

| Yes, Change Your Setting | No, Thanks |

....

NEW! **Profile Stats Pro:** See the full list of who's viewed your profile, and more. Upgrade now.

Profile Strength

While viewing your profile, not in edit mode, you can see how thorough

LinkedIn believes that your profile is. If your profile strength is lacking, edit your profile to provide more complete information.

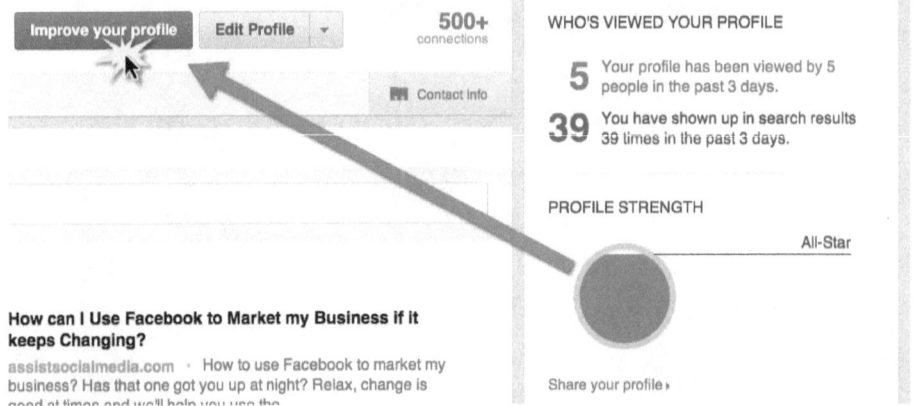

People Similar To

If you want to see others that have similar information in their LinkedIn profiles as the person you are viewing, you can view that in the top right of someone's profile. This can be a useful discovery method.

PEOPLE SIMILAR TO JASON

Phil Belleville
CEO at Local SEOd
Connect

People Also Viewed

When viewing your own profile or other's, you'll see who else the visitors also viewed. This can be a fantastic way to discover others in the related industry that you may want to connect with as well.

PEOPLE ALSO VIEWED

Jason Falls
Founder, Chief Instigator at Social Media Explorer

Mitch Joel
President at Twist Image

Scott Monty
Head of social media for Ford Motor Company [Note: I make connections only with people whom I have met]

In Common

You can see what you have in common with the person as well. This will review what groups, skills & experiences, or interests you have in common. Knowing your commonalities can make it easier to strike up conversation and interact online, as well as determining your intent of connecting with them.

IN COMMON WITH CHRIS

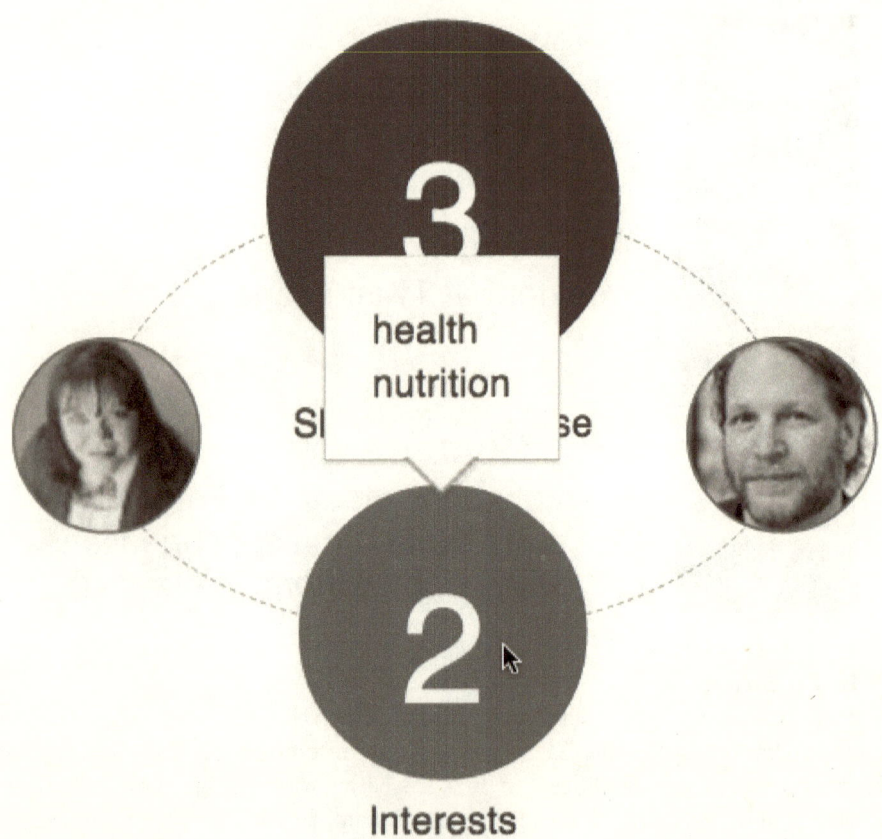

Multiple Language Profiles

While it would violate LinkedIn's user policy to have multiple accounts, it is possible to have multiple profiles if you need one in multiple languages. Depending upon what language and location other members are using will determine which version of your profile they see.

To create a profile in another language, select Edit on your profile:

Ask to be recommended

Create profile in another language

Share profile

Export to PDF

Manage public profile settings

All other settings in completing your profile will be similar to the first profile you made. The new profile will end in a slightly different unique profile like, such as http://linkedin.com/in/yourname/**es** for Spanish.

If you are viewing someone else's profile and wish to toggle to the alternate language, the lower right corner of their profile heading can switch.

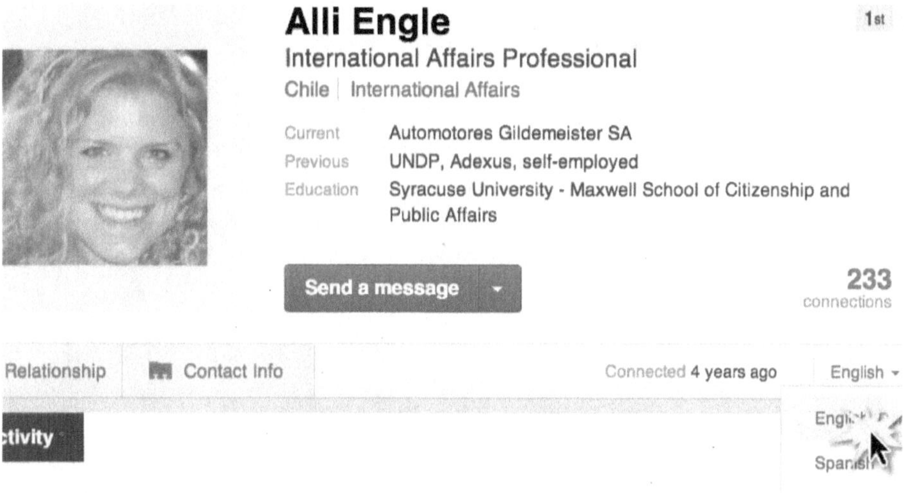

Alli Engle

1st

International Affairs Professional

Chile | International Affairs

Current   Automotores Gildemeister SA
Previous   UNDP, Adexus, self-employed
Education Syracuse University - Maxwell School of Citizenship and Public Affairs

Send a message ▾

233
connections

Relationship   Contact Info

Connected **4 years ago**   English ▾

English ▾

tivity

Spanish

If you are viewing your own profile and need to switch, the lower left under your profile photo will allow you to toggle between language profiles:

Alli Engle

International Affairs Professional

Chile | International Affairs

Current   Automotores Gildemeister SA

Previous   UNDP, Adexus, self-employed

Education   Syracuse University - Maxwell School of Citizenship and Public Affairs

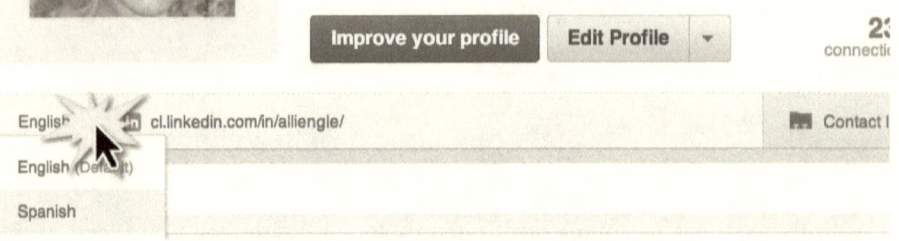

Remember, multiple accounts is in violation of the terms of service but multiple language profiles is acceptable.

For Your Website

Wether on your own website or for that of your company, you can include a profile overview from LinkedIn onto the website. Visit https://developer.linkedin.com/plugins#profile

Member Profile

Bring LinkedIn member profiles to your site to help users discover common professional connections.

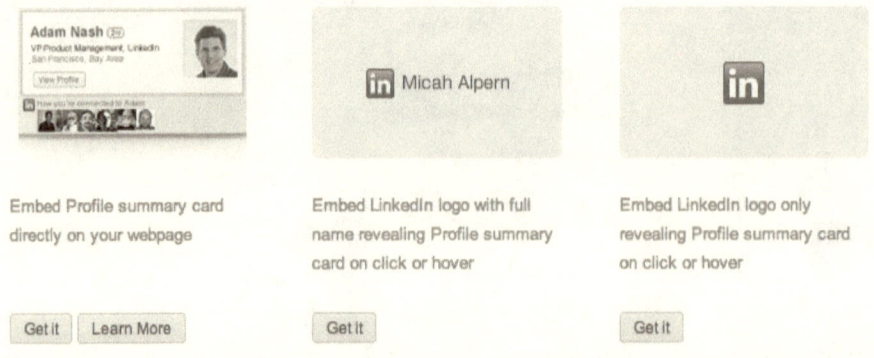

Embed Profile summary card directly on your webpage

Get it   Learn More

Embed LinkedIn logo with full name revealing Profile summary card on click or hover

Get it

Embed LinkedIn logo only revealing Profile summary card on click or hover

Get it

If you'd like a more thorough view of the profile, try this instead: https://developer.linkedin.com/plugins#full-member-profile

Full Member Profile

Bring full LinkedIn profiles to your site to display a person's professional background at-a-glance.

Make your site content richer by showing the summary, work experience and educational background for people featured on your site. Also, enable users to easily discover who they know in common, send a message, or establish a connection.

Learn more

ACCOUNT SETTINGS, PRIVACY, AND SECURITY

A vitally important aspect to managing any social media account is understanding and configuring your account settings, privacy, and security to meet your needs. To view your default settings, navigate to the Account & Settings.

If you are a paying member, this is also where to go for enabling the OpenLink and Premium Badge settings. Likewise, if you need more InMails, you can buy them here. Introductions are available on a per month basis as well.

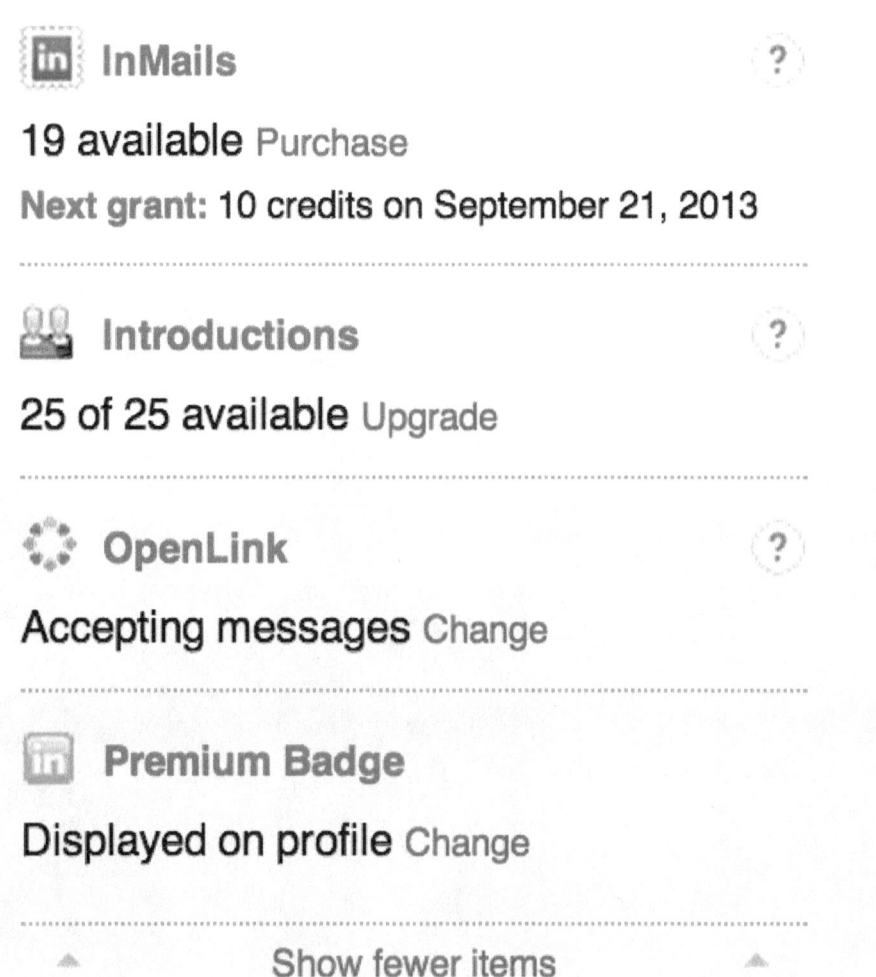

InMails ?

19 available Purchase

Next grant: 10 credits on September 21, 2013

Introductions ?

25 of 25 available Upgrade

OpenLink ?

Accepting messages Change

Premium Badge

Displayed on profile Change

▲ Show fewer items ▲

The payment options and levels of membership can be reviewed here as well.

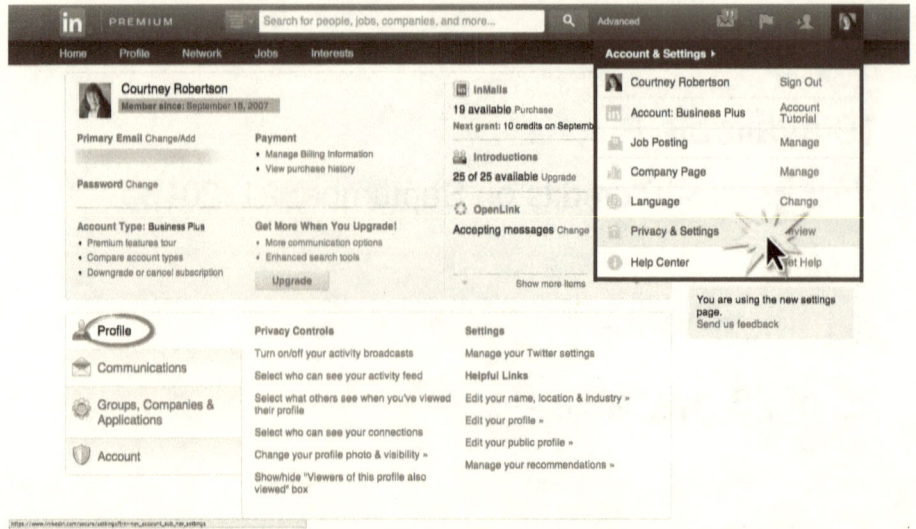

You'll be presented initially with settings regarding your profile. Notice that you can see when you've joined LinkedIn as well.

Privacy Controls

If you are job hunting but haven't yet notified your employer, it will be very important to modify your activity broadcasts. Let's review the options:

Privacy Controls

Turn on/off your activity broadcasts

Select who can see your activity feed

Select what others see when you've viewed their profile

Select who can see your connections

Change your profile photo & visibility »

Show/hide "Viewers of this profile also viewed" box

Activity broadcasts may be good to hide while you initially create your profile as to avoid excessive notifications to your contacts.

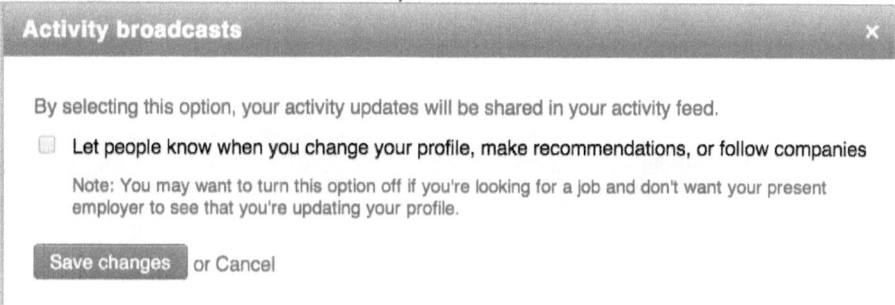

If you choose to allow others to see your activity on LinkedIn (a good idea most of the time), then you can specify who specifically can view your profile.

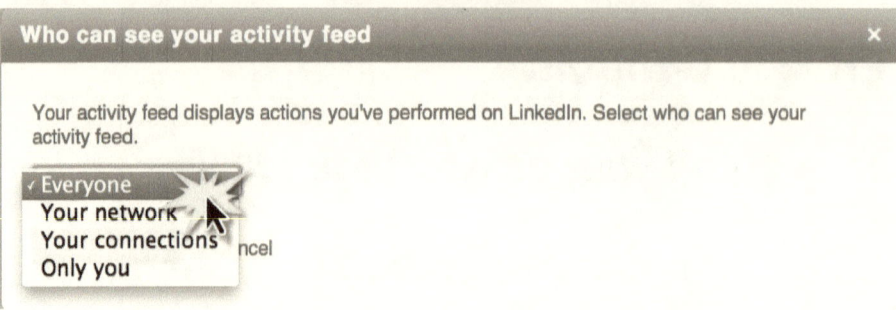

If you want to view someone else's profile without them knowing, you can remain anonymous. Most of the time I allow others to see that I've visited.

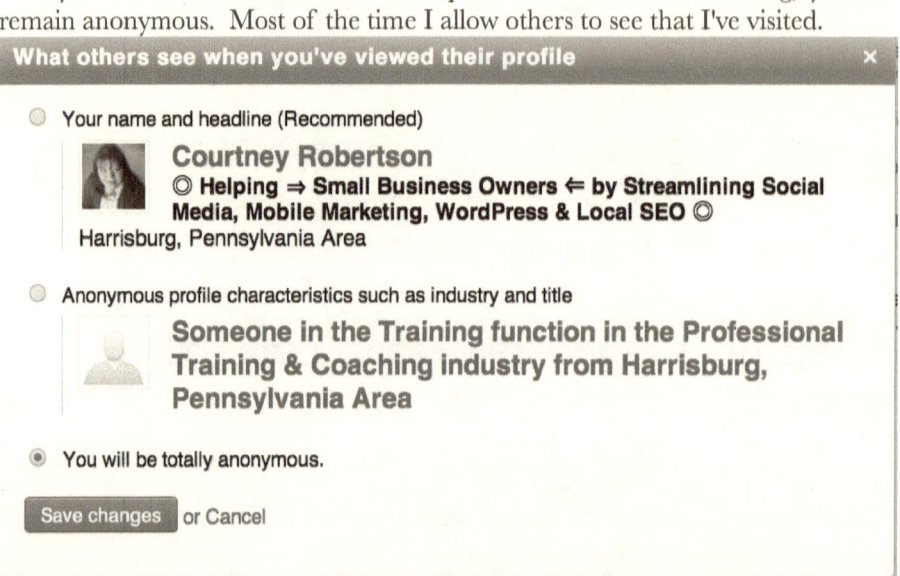

Do you want others to see who you have connected with? Often this is also good to do, as it helps them connect with others.

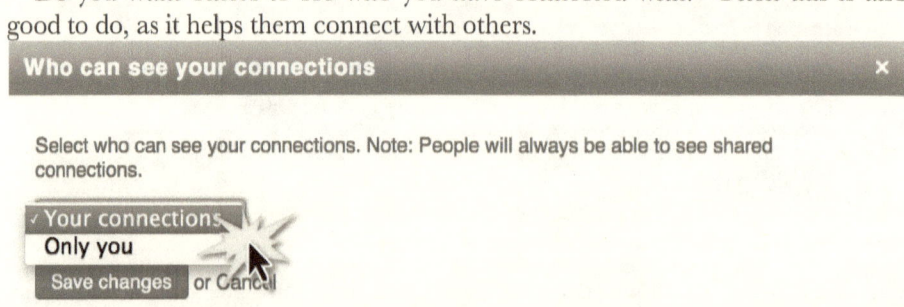

Need to update your profile photo? You can do this from your profile, or by visiting via settings. Likewise, you can control who can see your profile.

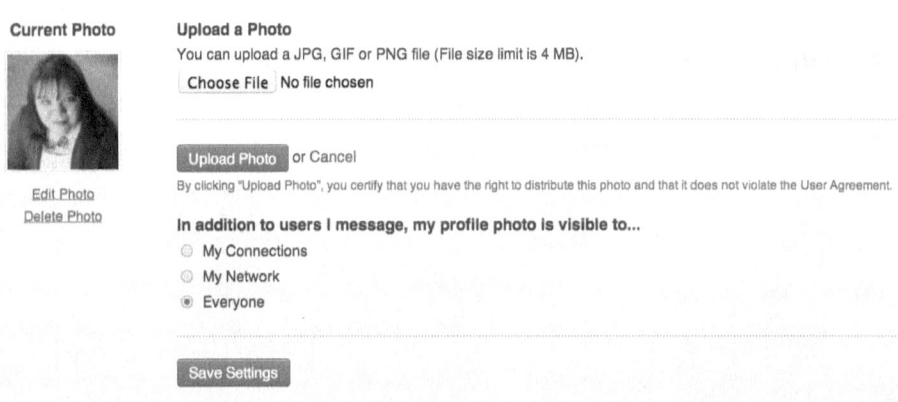

Additionally part of networking can also involve revealing other similar people that people also viewed. This fosters networking, so I keep this enabled.

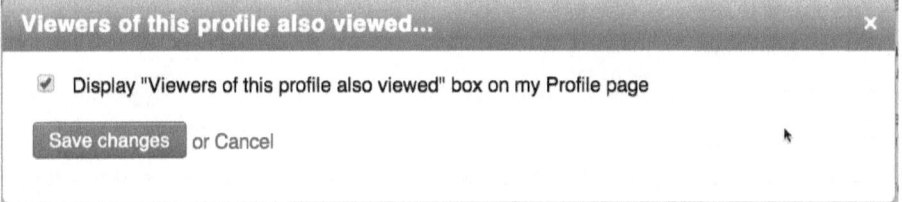

Communications

Is your email inbox getting too full of LinkedIn notifications? There's help to turn much of that off!

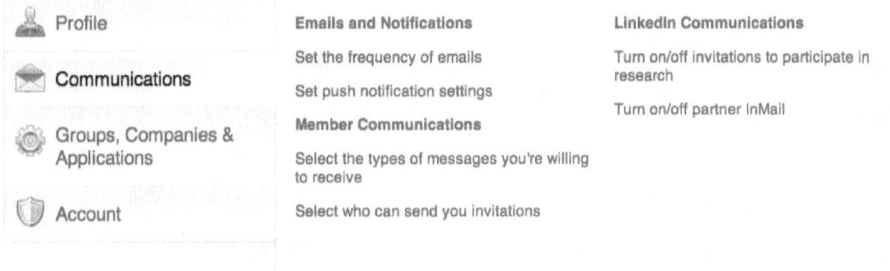

Once presented with Frequency settings, you can dig in deeper to multiple options:

Email frequency

Messages from other members
Invitations, messages, and other communication from LinkedIn members

Invitations to connect	Individual Email ⬍
Invitations to join groups	Individual Email ⬍
Messages from connections	Individual Email ⬍
InMails, introductions and OpenLink messages	No Email ⬍
New connection suggestions	Individual Email ⬍
Profiles sent to you	Individual Email ⬍
Job suggestions from connections	Individual Email ⬍

Save changes   Cancel

Email frequency

Messages from other members
Invitations, messages, and other communication from LinkedIn members

Updates and news
Summaries of what's happening in your network and topics you're following

Group digests
Summaries of what's happening in your groups

Notifications
Likes, comments, and other responses to your activity

Messages from LinkedIn
Insights and suggestions for getting the most out of LinkedIn

Go back to Settings

To change what settings create alerts on your mobile apps, review your push notification settings:

45

Push notification settings

Messages from other members
Invitations, messages and other communication from LinkedIn members

Notifications
Likes, comments, and other activity around you

Go back to Settings

To make your profile more discoverable to various people seeking connections, you can open up your profile for various opportunities. If you are not actively seeking any of these connections, no need to include them.

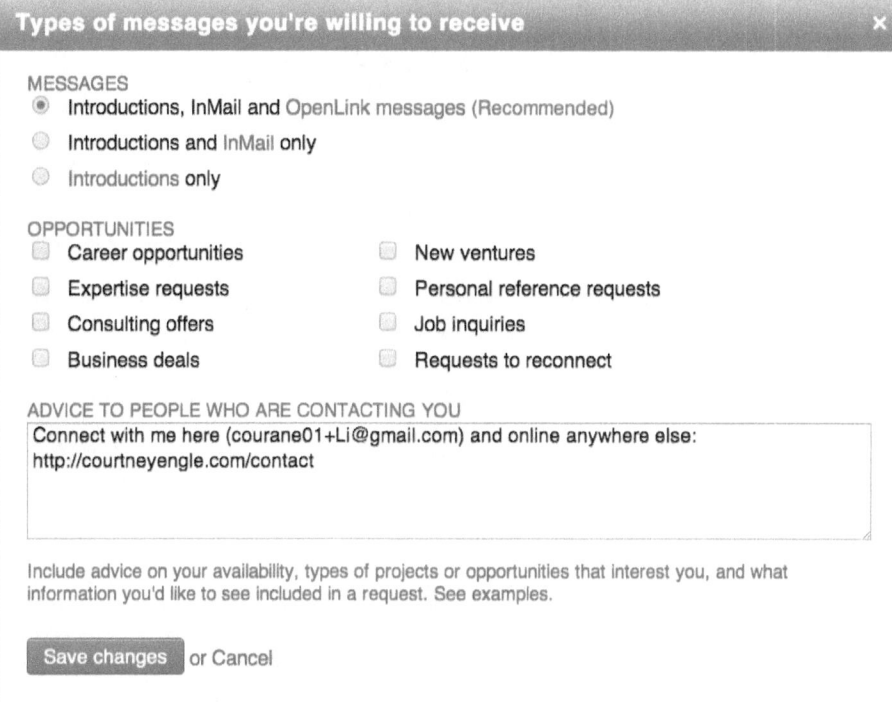

To specify who can send you invitations to connect, modify these settings:

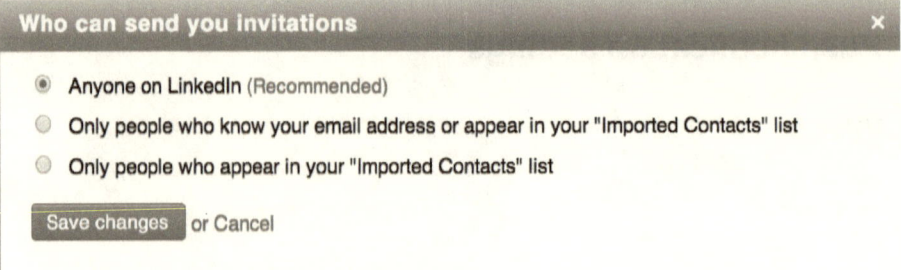

Groups, Companies, and Applications

From the Groups settings, you can organize which groups appear in which order and view the groups you have joined.

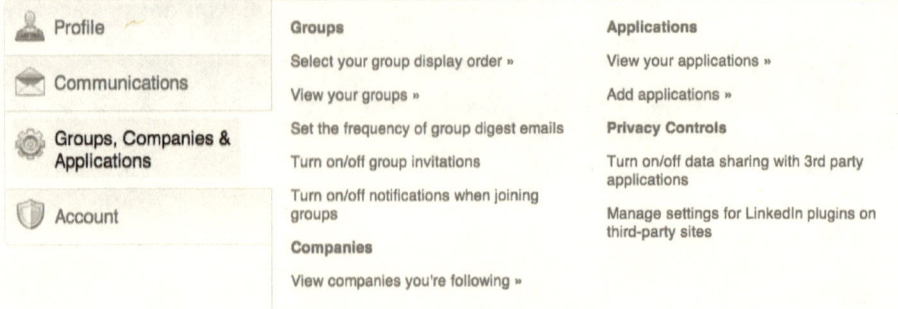

The amount of notifications I get from LinkedIn is minimal with the exception of groups. To turn that off or modify your settings:

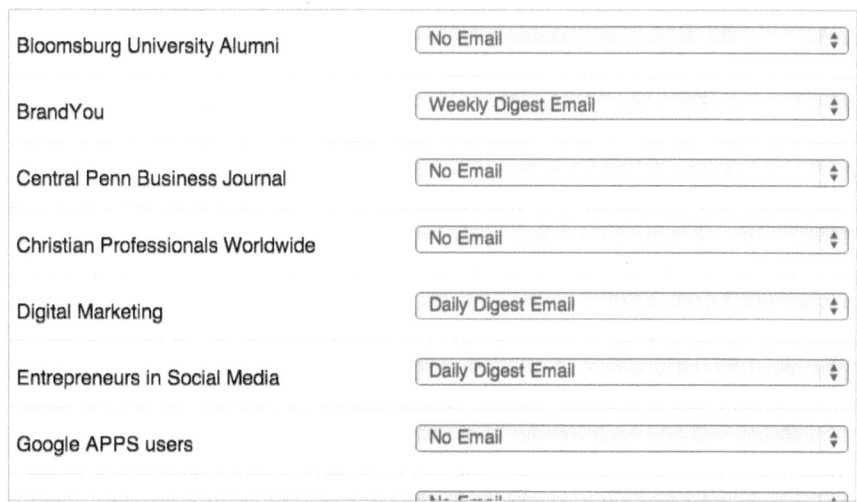

Note: Your changes will take effect within a few days.

Save changes or Cancel

If you find that you are invited to too many groups, turn that off:

Group invitations   x

☑ I am open to receiving group invitations.

Save changes or Cancel

Please see the "Set the frequency of messages" setting to determine how you would like to be notified of group invitations.

If you are actively joining groups to seek employment, you might want to disable others from seeing that.

Notifications when joining groups   x

☑ Yes, publish an update to my network whenever I join a group that has these notifications enabled by the group owner.

Save Changes or Cancel

Note: You may want to turn this option off if you're looking for a job and want to be more private about which groups you join.

You can also view the companies that you are following. this works much like the companies menu from above.

Finally, the apps connected to your profile are important to monitor. LinkedIn has retired its apps that show on your public profile, but still allows 3rd party systems to access your account. It is important to review what 3rd party systems you have authorized to connect with you account and delete any that you do not recognize or implement.

Authorized Applications

Applications

Listed here are the applications you have either installed or granted access to while you were using LinkedIn. Removing them here will remove them from your home page, profile page, and prevent any further access to your LinkedIn data. To remove them from your home page only, visit the home page and click the X on the application title bar. To remove them from your profile page only, visit the Edit My Profile page and click the Remove link next to the title of the application.

	Application Name	
☐	Polls by LinkedIn	about

External Websites

Listed here are external partner websites to which you have granted access to your LinkedIn profile and network data. If you remove that access here, they will no longer be able to access your LinkedIn data. To re-enable them in the future, visit the website and grant access again.

	Partner Name
☐	Business Exchange

Within your Account settings, you can modify your email address, change your password, upgrade your account, delete your account, change your photos, and more.

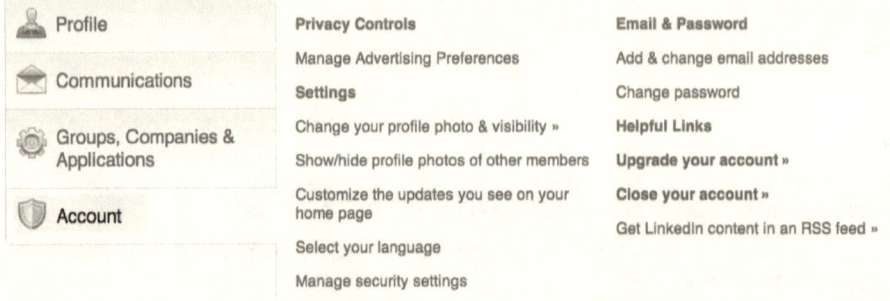

LinkedIn does allow you a little control over your advertising preferences. If you don't mind LinkedIn tracking you to show you ads on other websites, you can leave this enabled. I personally prefer any ads that I am served to be customized to me, but I also understand the privacy concerns people have. LinkedIn will not give your personal information to these websites.

Ads by LinkedIn - Overview

"Ads by LinkedIn" are advertisements shown to LinkedIn ... Read more

Ad selection

Ads shown to you are selected based on non-personally ... Read more

Protecting your personal information

LinkedIn does not directly share your personal information ... Read more

☑ LinkedIn may show me ads on third-party websites.

☑ LinkedIn may show me ads based on third party data.

Save changes or Cancel

In this same Account area, you can choose to turn off photos of others. I'm not sure when I'd opt to use this service, but it is interesting that we can do this.

Profile photos of other members   ✕

Select whose photos you would like to see.

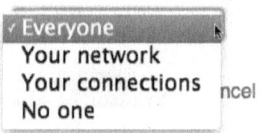

✓ Everyone
  Your network
  Your connections   ncel
  No one

If you'd like to customize what content you see in the updates on the main page, specify what things you'd like to turn off or on. If you hide anything, it will appear in the "Hidden" tab.

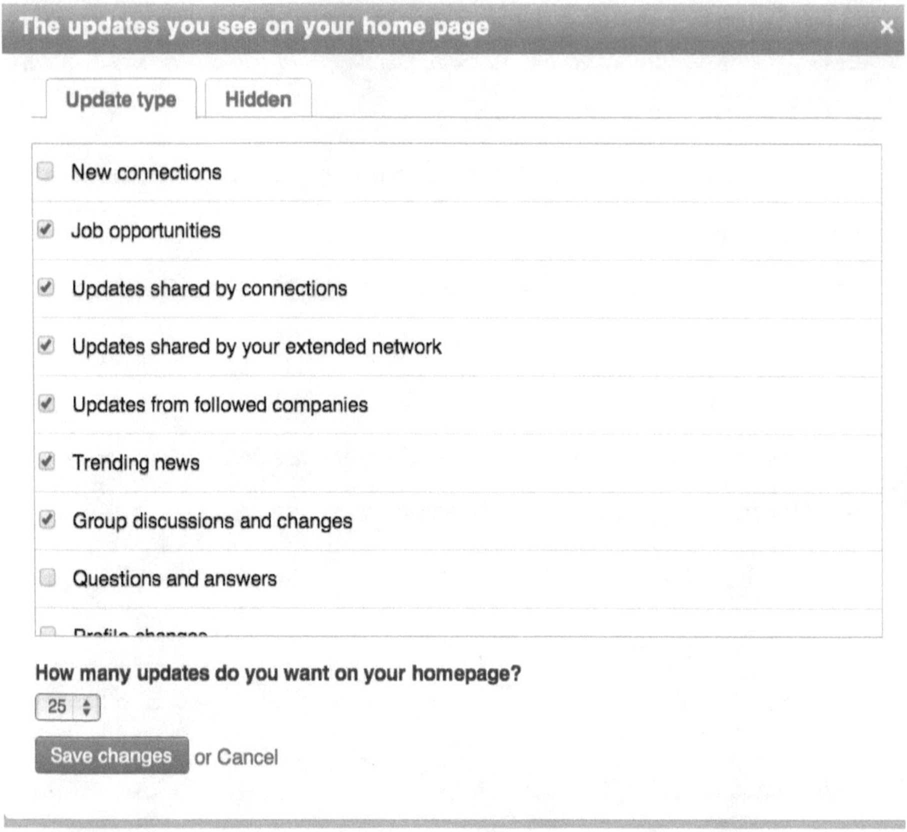

The updates you see on your home page ✕

| Update type | Hidden |

☐ New connections

☑ Job opportunities

☑ Updates shared by connections

☑ Updates shared by your extended network

☑ Updates from followed companies

☑ Trending news

☑ Group discussions and changes

☐ Questions and answers

☐ Profile changes

How many updates do you want on your homepage?

25 ▲▼

Save changes or Cancel

If you prefer to use LinkedIn in a different language, you can switch to any of the following:

Select your language ✕

Bahasa Indonesia	Français	Português
Bahasa Malaysia	한국어	Română
čeština	Italiano	Русский
Dansk	Nederlands	Svenska
Deutsch	日本語	Tagalog
English	Norsk	Türkçe
Español	Polski	

One of the most important settings that you can manage is your security settings. By enabling "Secure connection" you will be using the httpS protocol when navigating the website, which is more secure.

Two-step verification is incredibly valuable. If your account is logged in to from an unknown device, you will get an email at your primary account email on file. It will also log out any other locations currently logged in during this first switch.

Security Settings

Secure connection

☐ A secure connection will be used when you are browsing LinkedIn. Learn More >

Note: Some LinkedIn applications **will not** be available when you select this option.

Two-step verification for sign-in

Turning this feature on will sign you out anywhere you're currently signed in. We will then require you to enter a verification code the first time you sign in with a new device or LinkedIn mobile application. Learn More >

Currently OFF • Turn On

Note: Some LinkedIn applications **will not** be available when you select this option.

Done

GROWING YOUR NETWORK

Building your network is vital to your business, but knowing your intentions and directing those into areas of focus is what will produce results. While many have joined LinkedIn in particular, few have maintained the rapport with connections after acquiring the next job. To really create the maximum impact, make time to network as part of your ongoing business routine.

There are two schools of thought regarding LinkedIn connections. The first and more traditional approach is to only connect to others that you would give an endorsement of their skills. Connections should be exclusive to those that you have met in some capacity, whether online or off. This is the original intent of LinkedIn, but as social media has evolved, this approach is fading.

Open networking is the second approach. In the Open Networking method, people are happy to connect with each other and build a business relationship from interacting solely on LinkedIn. I practice this approach and only resist connecting with others when the accounts seem to be entirely self-promotional or I know by experience that I would not wish to endorse or encounter this person in offline networking.

Open Networkers can be easily identified by glancing through their profiles. You'll notice paying members are denoted by a gold LinkedIn logo. If they too are open networkers, you'll see a circle to indicate as such.

Courtney (Engle) Robertson
◎ Helping ⇒ Small Business Owners ⇐ by Streamlining Social Media, Mobile Marketing, WordPress & Local SEO ◎

Chambersburg, Pennsylvania | Professional Training & Coaching

Current	Simple Local Business, Timao Multimedia
Previous	Social Mobile Local Marketing Pros, GFYDMember.com, Web20iGo
Education	Shippensburg University of Pennsylvania

Edit Profile ▾

500+
connections

Other signs of being an open networker can include

- TopLinked.com and it's associated group http://www.linkedin.com/groups?gid=42031
- LION500.com and it's associated group http://www.linkedin.com/groups?gid=92107
- Mentions of LION in their profile (Linked In Open Networkers)
- A person's email address in their contact information

Those that are truly practicing Open Networking will value your connection effort, but this is really a scattershot approach. If you are open to connecting with others in this manner, it is common curtesy to accept their invites to connect promptly. There is a set limit of invites users can send out, and not acting upon the request hinders the other person.

Let's begin building the network by looking for those you already know. LinkedIn can scan many email systems for your contacts. In your Connections, scan your email address book, but do so with caution. When you grant LinkedIn permission to access your address book on any of the leading webmail services or software platforms, it will ask if you wish to invite all of them to connect. Be careful with this. It is very helpful to give LinkedIn your address so that you can find connections, but there is no need to spam people not yet on LinkedIn. In addition, if you maintain an email list, LinkedIn will allow you to upload an export of that list in a .csv format.

YOUR CONTACTS

Contacts

Building your network of connections is vital to your experience on LinkedIn. The more connections that you have, the more your profile will be discovered. Once you've built a complete profile, it is time to connect with those that you already know. Browse to Contacts.

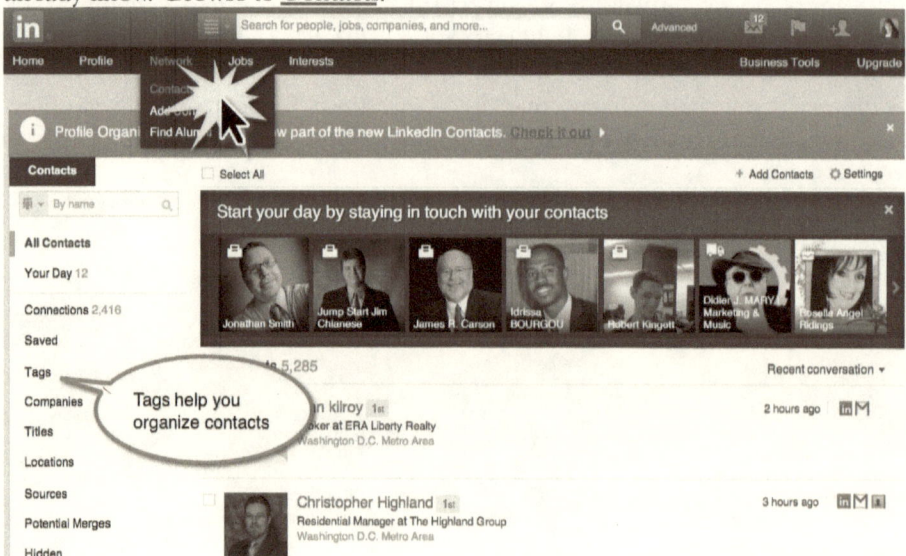

Add Connections

To add new contacts, go to add connections:

Get started by adding your email address.

Your email

courane01@gmail.com

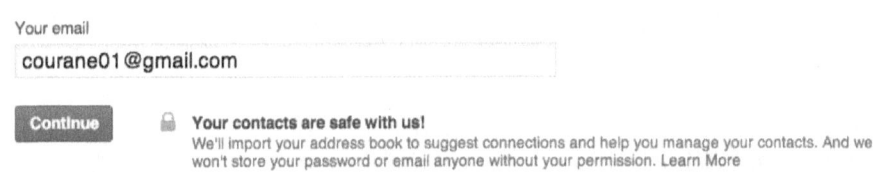

Or from Contacts, sync email contacts:

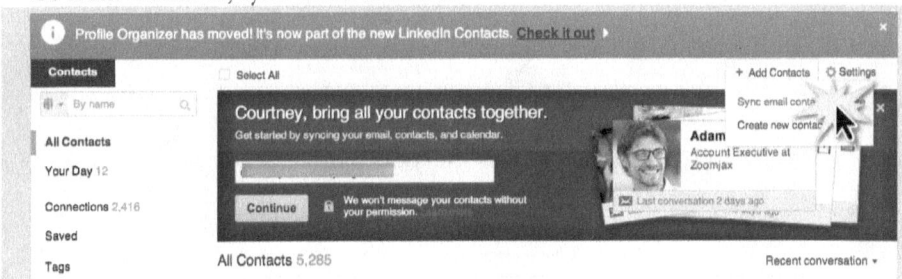

Add Connections   Remove Connections

If you are using a common email provider, like Gmail, you can scan that address book. Each service may request that you grant permission for the accounts to connect together.

The site **www.linkedin.com** is requesting access to your Google Account for the product(s) listed below.

✉ **Email address**

M **Gmail**

📅 **Google Calendar**

📇 **Google Contacts**

Google is not affiliated with www.linkedin.com, and we recommend that you grant access only if you trust the site.

If you grant access, you can revoke access at any time under 'My Account'. www.linkedin.com will not have access to your password or any other personal information from your Google Account. Learn more

Grant access   **Deny access**

If you do not have any of the listed email providers, you can still upload a listing of contacts. Go to "Any Email", and chose to upload a contacts file. This would also be a great way to upload members of your email newsletter. Note: I do not recommend mass inviting people. At this point all we want is to provide LinkedIn with our email address book, not to connect quite yet.

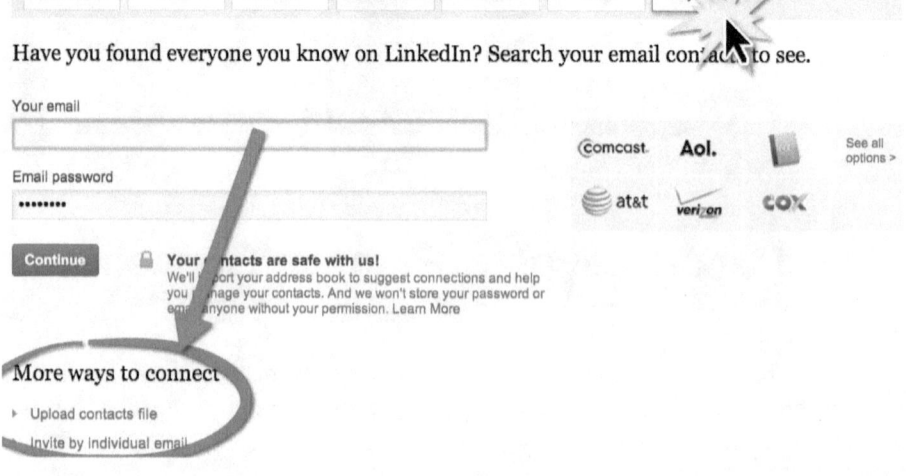

If you need further help with how to upload a .csv file that you've exported, see LinkedIn's Help.

Remove Contacts

If you ever find yourself in the position of not wanting to remain connected to someone, you can remove them. To do this, go to Contacts, select "more" in the bottom of the profile, and Remove Connections.

Mari Smith 1st

Social Media Speaker at Mari Smith I Social Media

Greater San Diego Area

● Tag   ✉ Message   More ▾

Hide

john kilroy 1st

Broker at ERA Liberty

Washington D.C. Metro Area

Remove

Invited Imported Contacts

I strongly advise the slightly tedious process of customizing your invitation to connect. For that reason, only once LinkedIn as our entire email address book do I recommend sorting through Imported Contacts. Browse to each person you'd like to connect with. If they are already on LinkedIn, they'll have a blue logo icon on the right side of the imported list. Select these people first as they are already using LinkedIn. If they do not have that icon, then you are additionally inviting them to join the network. This can be helpful on rare occasions, but is generally not appreciated to send to all your contacts.

Compose a unique message for each new connection that you invite. The default message requesting to connect demonstrates you are only interested in amassing numbers of connections rather than furthering an authentic relationship. Send your invites one at a time and subtly remind the person how you met elsewhere.

Profile Organizer

LinkedIn's Profile Organizer is available to paying members. It is ideal for those in human resources, recruiting, or related to the hiring process especially. While this once stood apart from Contacts, LinkedIn has merged the features into the Contacts area. Additional fields of information are available for storing details about your connections and sorting them based upon your needs, such as saving contacts for later viewing. To view these, visit a profile of one of your connections and view the additional fields below their profiles.

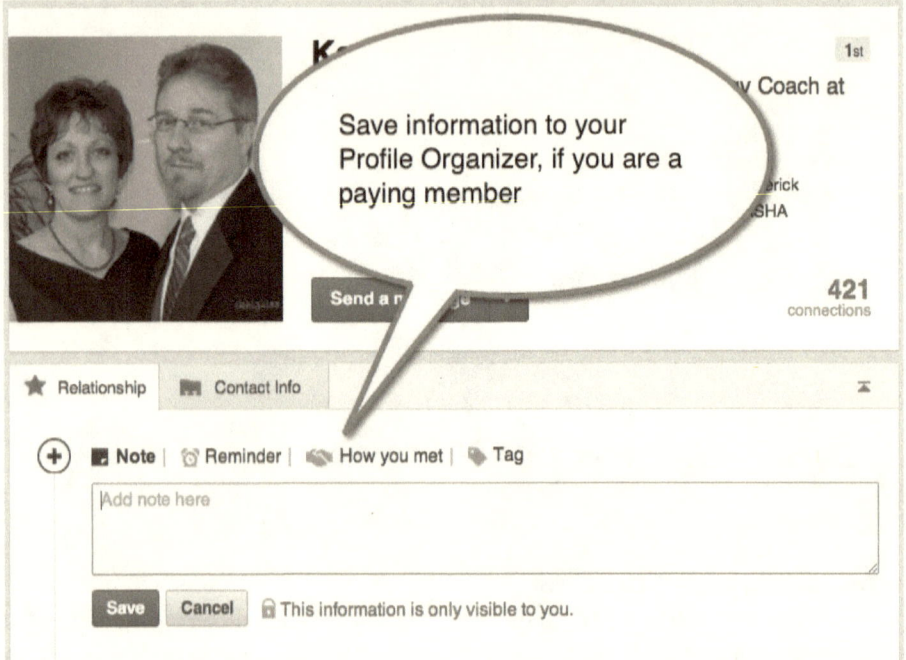

If you are viewing a profile that you are not yet connected with, you can save this person to your "Saved" connections by selecting the star on their profile.

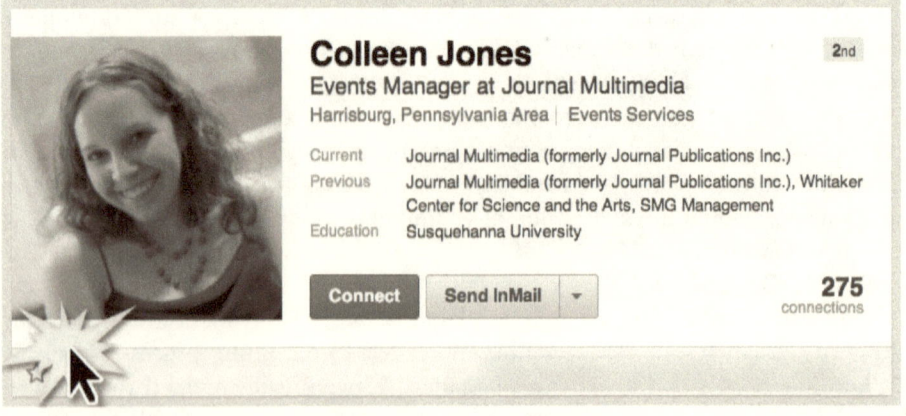

Organizing Contacts with Tags

While not a perfect substitution for Profile Organizer, you can organize how you know people by using tags. From Network, Contacts, on the left, see Tags to view those who you have assigned Tags to. Organizing these as you build your network is ideal, though it can be handled whenever you like. To assign tags, view all contacts and select "Tags" under their profile, or by visiting their profiles and seeing the extra fields under their Headline.

All Contacts 5,132

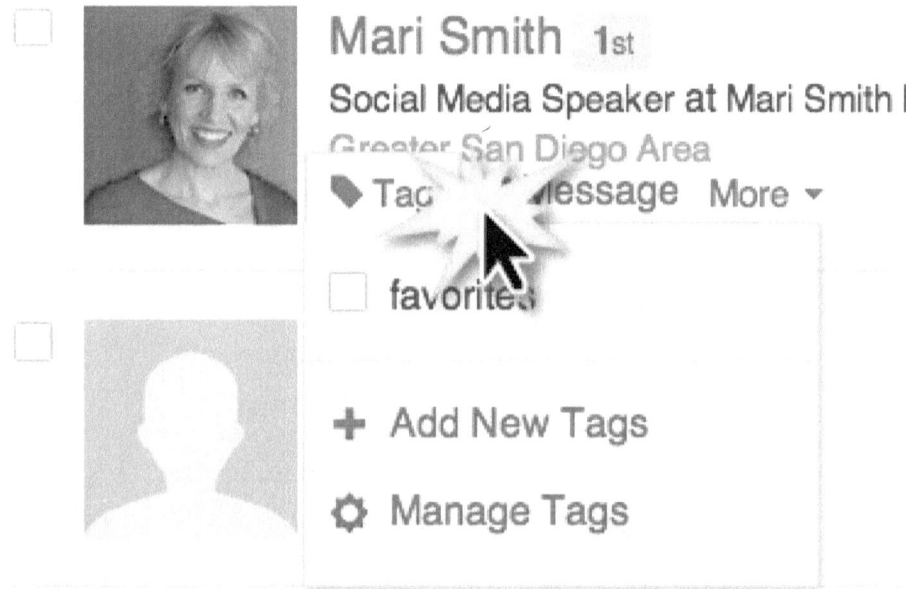

College Connections

In addition to scanning your contacts from your address book, you can search LinkedIn for college alumni. This can be a wealth of information on all other data included in their profile. View Network, Find Alumni.

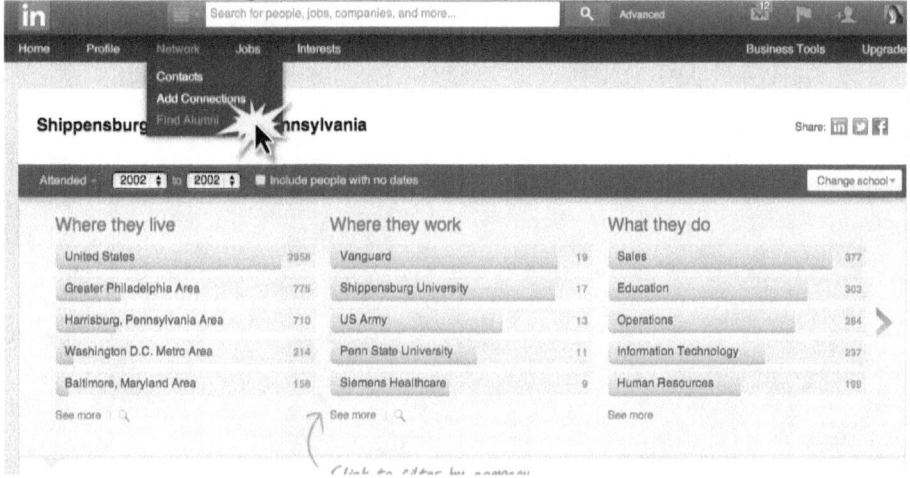

As you build your network of contacts, the important thing to remember is that you are not just collecting connections. You are building these connections so that you can refer business to each other, interact on their status updates, and give recommendations. LinkedIn isn't a place to sit back and watch what everyone else does, but a meaningful way to further your offline networking. Your goal is to definitely connect with many people, whether you meet them in person at a chamber mixer event or you have mutual contacts and have never met in person. Ultimately, you are here to be helpful and to meet those that you might want to conduct business with in the future. Finding initial connections is just the beginning. Remembering to connect with others after each networking event or conference you've attended is vital, and engaging on content shared as well as sharing relevant information will help you build ongoing relationships.

GROUPS

Joining Groups

To further your reach and expand your networking opportunities, joining groups can be a huge help. Some groups are worth joining because they are just large. Large groups can help you expand your connections because other group members can see your profile or inbox email you, even if you aren't connected together directly. However, you'll want a good mix of joining big groups for expanding your network and joining professional groups or even interest and region based groups as well. You have up to 50 groups that you can be a part of, including administrating a group.

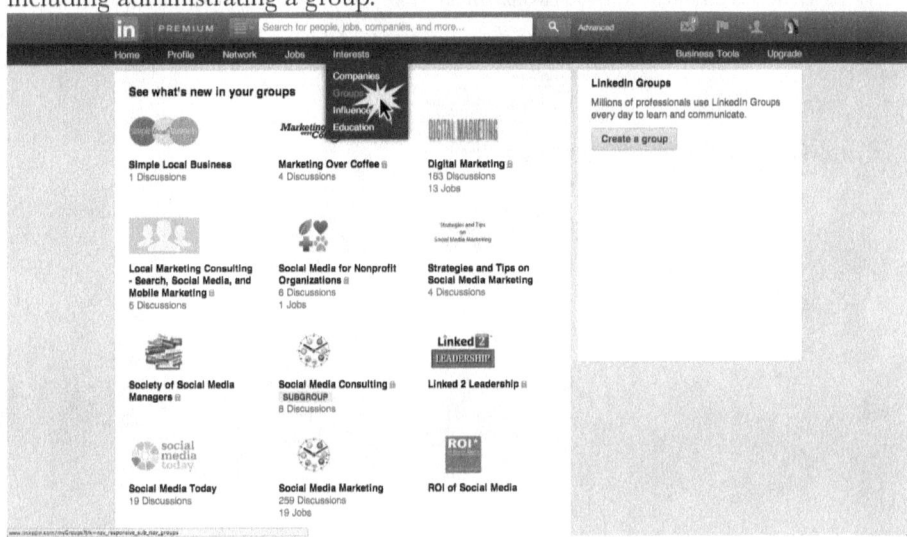

Before joining groups, let's develop a strategy for which groups you'll join and why. Write the follow answers down before joining any groups:

1. What words are your ideal clients search for?
2. Who do you want to meet? What titles do they hold and what companies do they work for?
3. What professional, trade, or alumni organizations do you belong to?
4. What hobbies and interests do you have?

5. What platforms are you using in your business that you might want help learning?
6. What region do you live in or serve? Or where do you want to move to or expand services to?

Next, navigate to Groups You May Like. You can see this widget on your LinkedIn dashboard, or by going to Groups and scrolling to the very bottom.

From the main dashboard on the right side:

GROUPS YOU MAY LIKE

 **Innovations in Social Media Marketing**

✪ **Join** - Professional Group

 **SEO and Social Media Marketing Tips and Secrets**

✪ **Join** - Professional Group

Social Media Tool Coaching

✪ **Join** - Professional Group

Feedback I See more »

Groups You May Like evaluates the content in your profile as well as looking at what groups those in your network are members of.

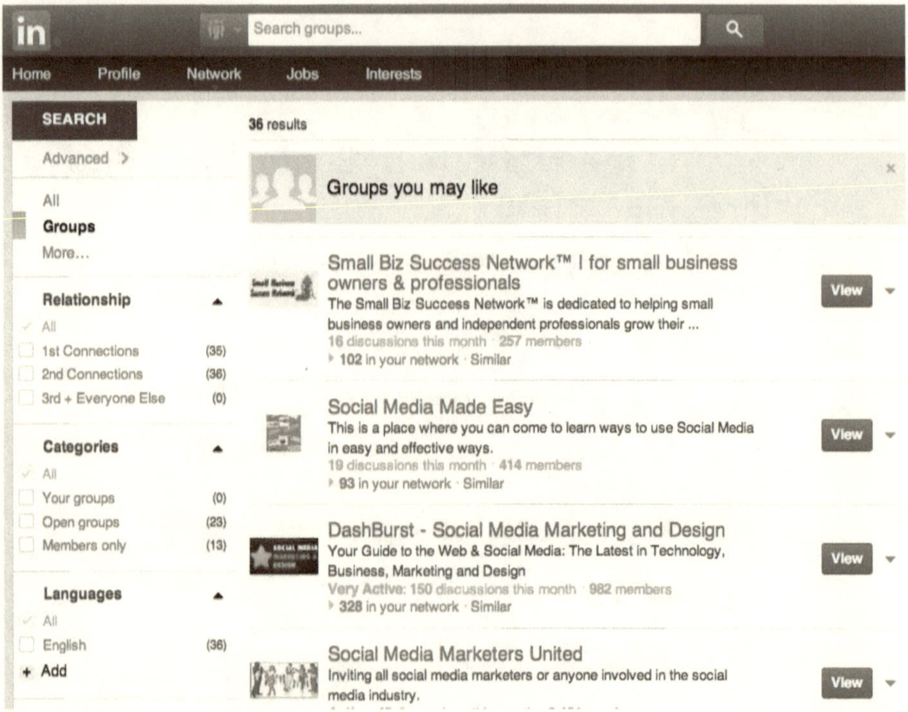

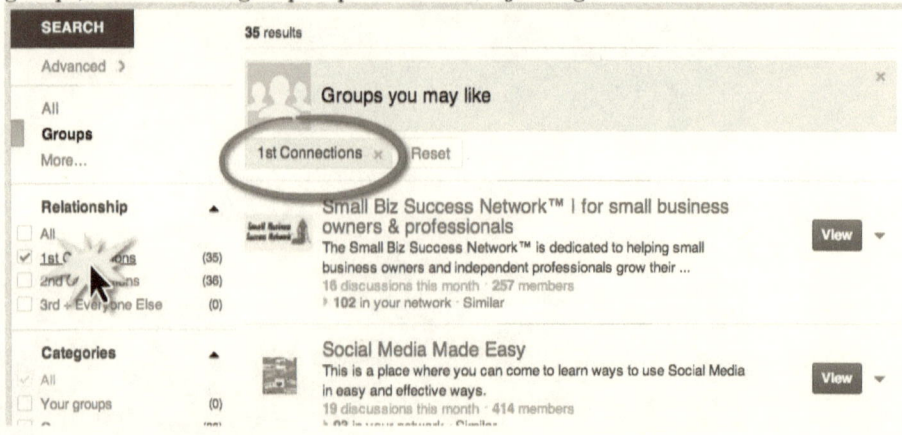

On the left side you can narrow down the results. You can specify that you want "Open Groups" to indicate you only want to see groups that you can join, or see groups that only your network of connections are members of. You can turn off your filtered search results, see what connections you have within a groups, and view the group to preview before joining.

Groups Directory

The <u>Groups Directory</u> looks very much like "Groups You May Like" but excludes the automatic search of your profile. To view it, see "Groups You May Like" and select Groups on the left, with no additional search filters displayed. The largest groups will appear first in the list.

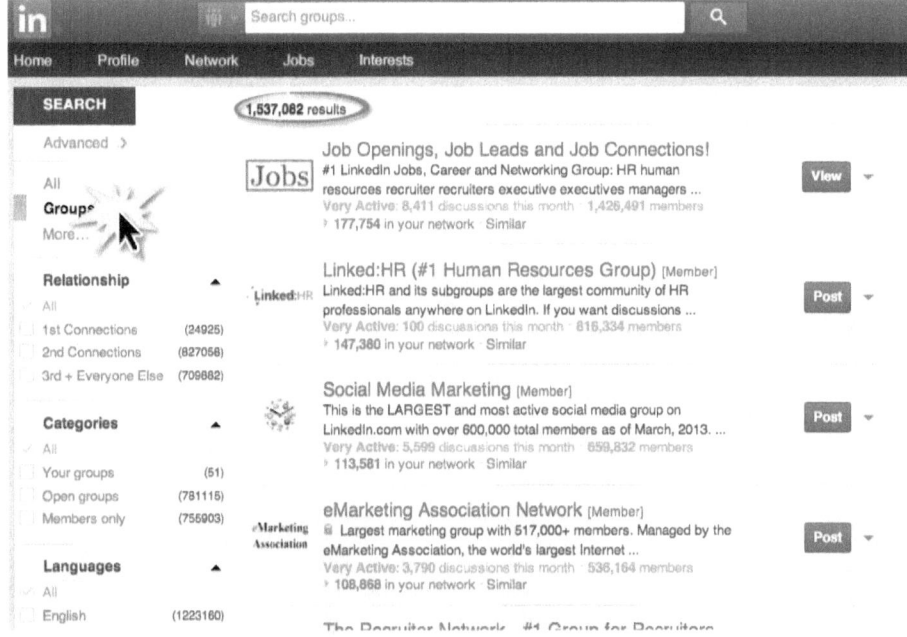

Search for those keywords that you wrote earlier, regions, alumni networks, and other organizations. Search also for the name of your city.

Open vs. Members Only Groups

LinkedIn explains the difference between open groups and members-only groups as:

The main difference is who can see the discussions. Members-only group discussions can only be seen by other group members. Open group discussions can be seen by anyone on the web and can be shared on other social networking platforms.

In members-only groups:

- There's a padlock icon next to the group name.
- You must be a LinkedIn member to join.
- Discussions won't show up in search engine results.
- Discussions are visible to group members only.
- The group manager has the option to switch to an open group. This change can only be made once and cannot be undone. Members are notified if the group is switched to an open group.

In open groups:

- There isn't a padlock icon next to the group name.
- You must be a LinkedIn member to join.
- Discussions created before switching to an open group are archived and

visible to group members only.

- Discussions created after switching to an open group are searchable and visible to anyone on the web.
- Discussions can be shared using social networking sites like Twitter and Facebook.

Group managers have the option to allow LinkedIn members who aren't group members to contribute.

Greater **Chambersburg** Ch

 As the largest business organizatic
Commerce is the front door of the gre
Active: 22 discussions this month ·
▼ **Susan Kay Mason** and **112** in you

Susan Kay Mason
Marketing Consultant at Scor

 **Daniel Gaither**
Sales & Leasing Consultant

Groups Layout

As you view groups, there are some important areas in the layout to watch.

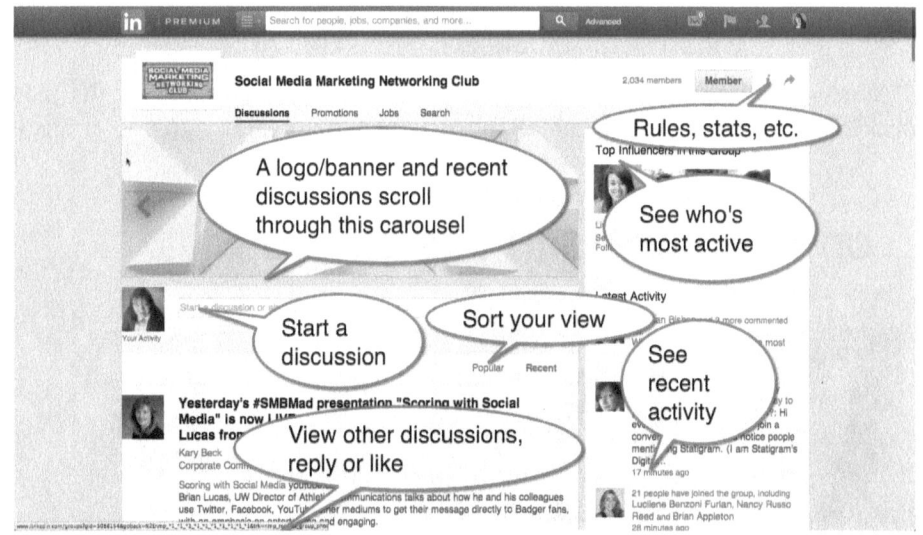

You can switch your view to see the most recent activity, or the default "popular" which shows content that is most actively engaged (likes, replies, or shares).

Discussions

When viewing a specific update, you have a few options. You can like or comment, which other networks like Facebook and Google+ also permit, flag something as a promotion or inappropriate, as well as get a link to the specific update to share with others by clicking on the discussion topic. You can also follow the update to be notified of additional comments about this update.

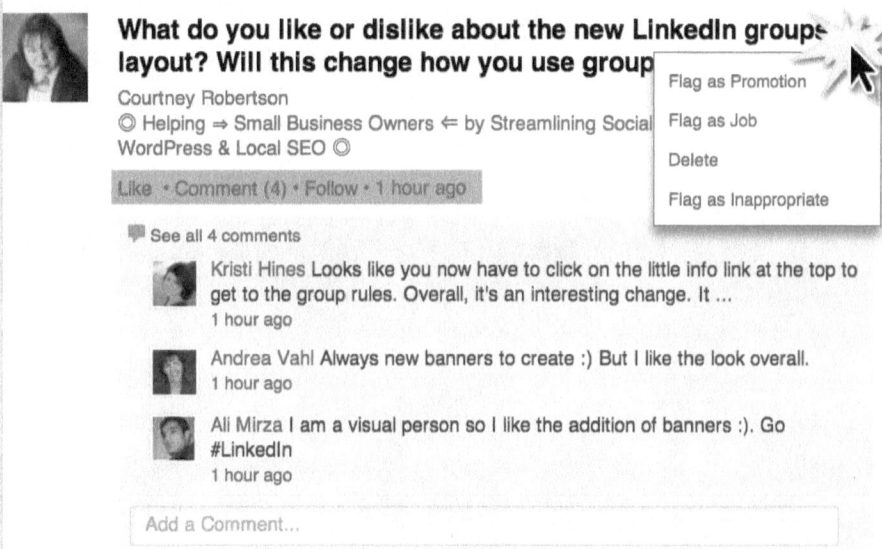

Also on the Group home page, you can see the top influencers of the past week. These are highly engaged members of the group, and may be a strategy you'd like to implement for a few key groups.

Top Influencers in this Group

Kristi Hines

Freelance Writer ★ Ghostwriter ★ Blog Content Writer ★ Promotional Strategist ★ Local Search Marketing Consultant   See all members ▶
Follow Kristi

You'll also see the latest updates as well. This is just a quick preview of what updates are currently happening, and great for readers that see Group pages from the default mode.

Latest Activity

 Kristi Hines and 3 more commented on:
The most important part of a great blog
is _____?
2 minutes ago

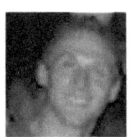 Brian Appleton started a discussion:
Looking for a Partner in my company for
Social Media & Blogging
4 minutes ago

 Damien Franco and 2 more commented
on:
Press releases on blog?
4 minutes ago

See all activity ▶

LinkedIn explains the Promotions tab as: gives group members a place to post their product promotions. Promotions don't expire, but they can be deleted by the poster or by a group owner/manager. This would be the place to announce your latest offer or share links. I'm not sure that many people are watching this part of groups, nor is sharing links scattershot across groups a good strategy.

Likewise, LinkedIn Groups can have a Jobs tab, which is up to the group moderator to create. LinkedIn explains these as: "A *Jobs* tab gives group members a place to share jobs and jobs discussions. Jobs discussions are automatically removed after 14 days. You can always post a job on LinkedIn if you want to reach a wider audience or need a job posted longer."

Determine Which Groups Are Worth It

As you preview the group, ask yourself a few more questions:

1. What are the group rules (see the top right corner). Do the members in the group honor the rules? If not, the moderator and owner aren't tuned in.
2. What discussions are members posting? Are they solely self-promotional or do they spark engagement and responses?
3. View the additional tabs that are relevant for you and this group. Are they being implemented?
4. How are the group statistics? Do these stats look like an active group (with lots of comments) or have the job titles of people you'd like to connect with?

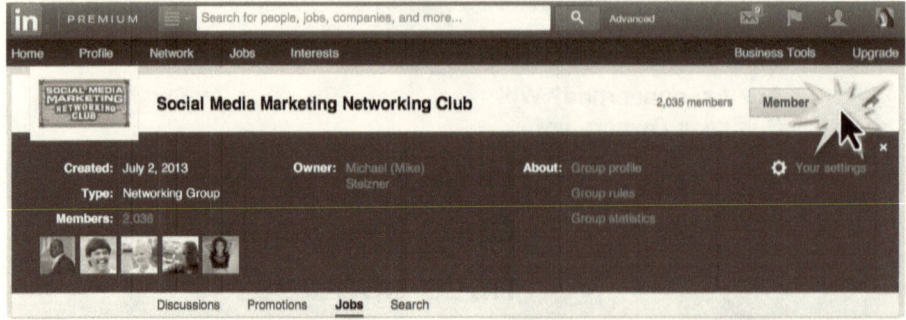

To review the group statistics:

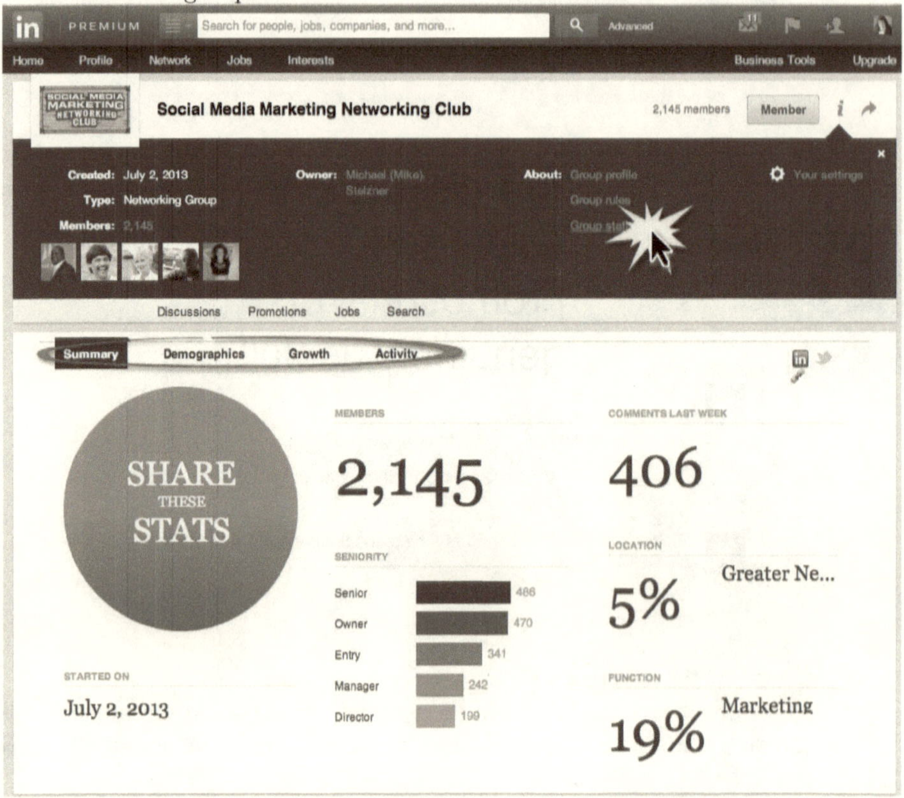

Once you've found a group that you feel is worth your while, have read the rules, and have a basic idea of how this group fits in with your strategy, join the group.

Joining Large Groups

Strategically joining a few large groups to maximize your search result exposure can be beneficial. To learn which groups are the largest, conduct a search on the groups directory. Leave the search box empty and click search. The largest groups will be displayed first.   **73**

A few large groups that you may want to join include:
1.   Jobs - especially if you are either seeking employment or hiring others
2.   Linked:HR - again good for finding employment or recruiting
3.   TopLinked - if you are an open networker. See also http://toplinked.com
4.   Lion500 - if you are an open networker

Select a few large groups with the sole purpose of expanding your network and being discovered. Remember you likely will not be using these groups to participate, but solely to be discovered in further search results.

Group Notification Settings

Like every social network, you can control how often LinkedIn emails you with updates. Visit each group's settings to control how often you receive emails, if non-members can see this group on your profile, and if group managers or other members can message you. You will want to allow other group members to message you. This is one of the main benefits of joining groups is the ability to message members within groups even without being connected.

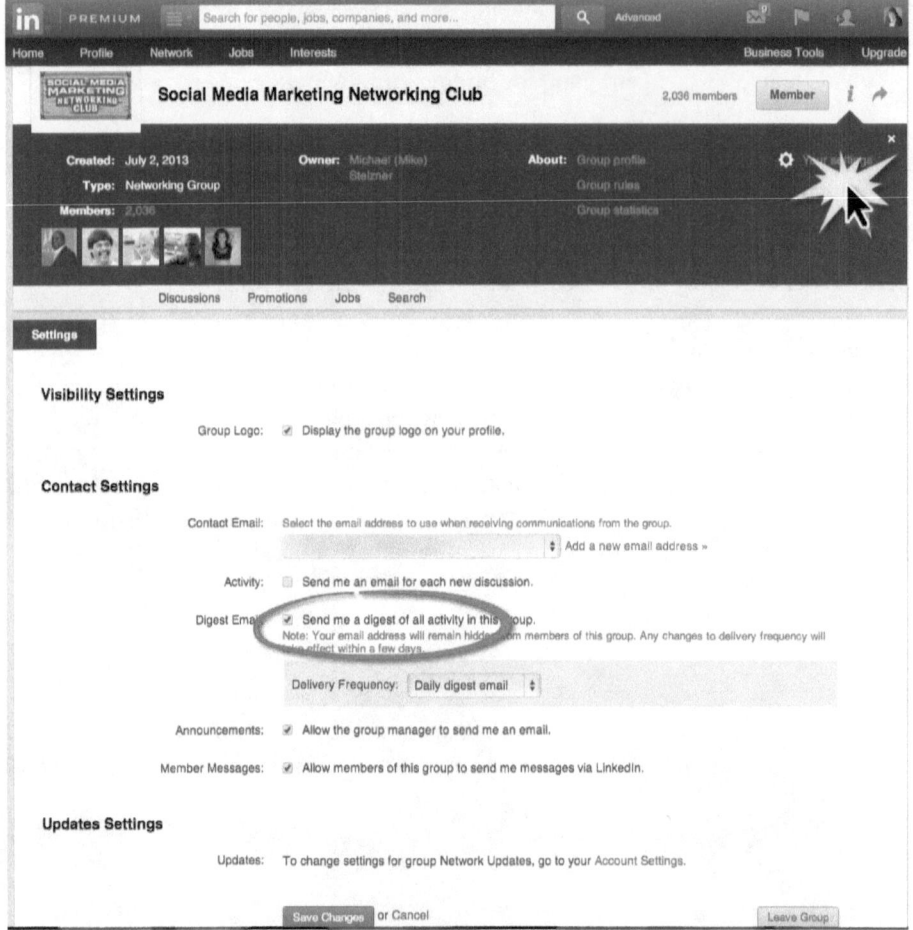

Creating a Group

Creating a group can quickly position you as networking connector, an expert in your field, or be a way to facilitate additional opportunities within your company. Plan your group thoroughly before creating it by asking yourself the following questions:

1. What will you name it? Use keywords that the community you'd like to build would be searching for
2. What type of group will this be? (Alumni, Corporate, Conference, Networking, Nonprofit, or Professional)
3. What will your logo be? It needs to be eye-catching in a tiny horizontal rectangle
4. Who will moderate the group and how often will moderation happen?
5. How can you promote this group?
6. What content will you share and how often to create discussion?

7. Do you want to approve all members before they can join, or allow the settings to be more open?
8. Do a search for the keywords you plan to use. How are other groups using those words in their summary, group description, and group names? What activity of those groups do you like and what would you differently?
9. What will your group rules be? Who will enforce them?

Once you've got your plan in mind for the purpose of your group, it's time to set the group up.

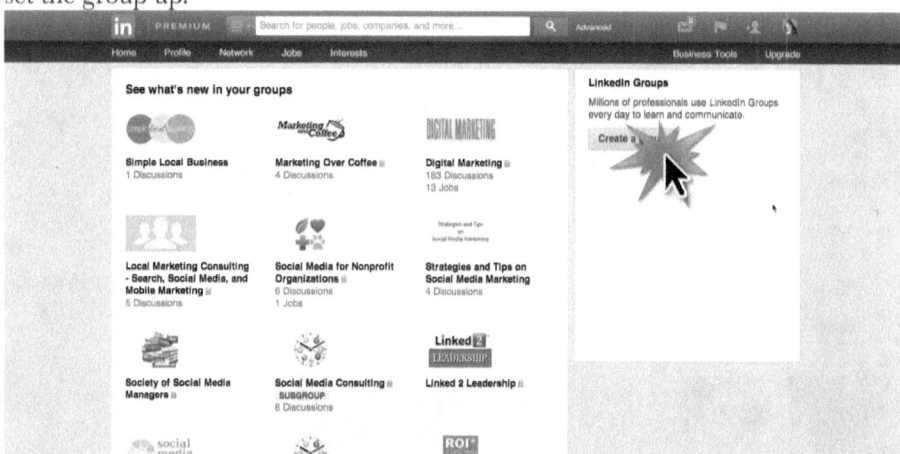

Upload your logo, but bear in mind that the 100 x 50 or 60 x 30 pixels sizes are needed. These group logos are intended to be small, and need to really pop well. Select your group type carefully, then enter in keyword rich summary and descriptions of your group. If you chose to include a website for the group, consider using a specific page like yoursite.com/linkedingroup to share custom information related to new members of the group. Take advantage of the group being listed in the Groups Directory, as well as other members showing it on their profiles to increase your exposure. Likewise, allow members to invite others to the group. Note to that within the location settings, you can specify your local region to narrow down groups such as your town's networking organizations.

Moderating Groups

LinkedIn's Group moderation settings are fairly robust. You'll now have access to a manage tab within the groups you moderate to display more possibilities.

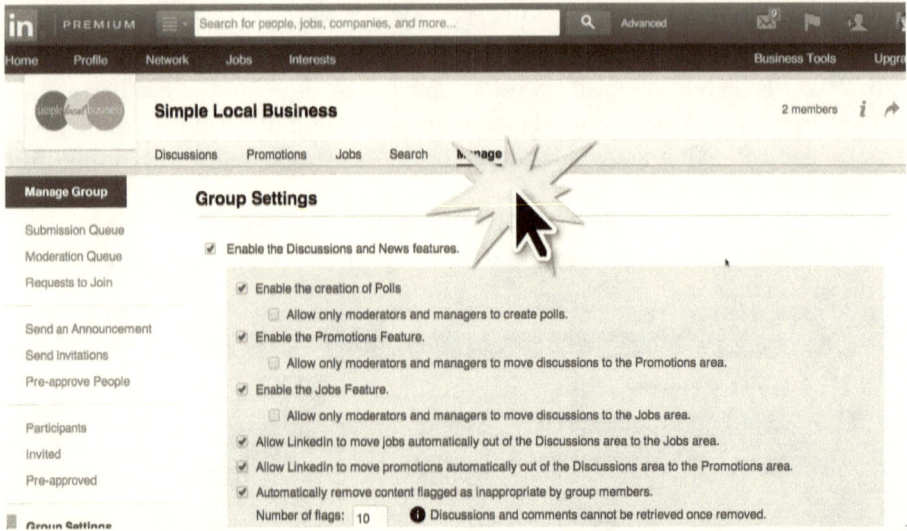

Once in the "Manage" area of your group, you'll notice additional options on the left column.

Manage Group

Submission Queue

Moderation Queue

Requests to Join

LinkedIn <u>defines</u> the "Submission Queue": allows your group management team to preview content posted by members before it's displayed or deleted from the group. If you've chosen that members must submit content before it is approved, then all content will land in the Submission Queue. You can go through to identify each item and move it to the appropriate tab.

Moderation Queue is different though. LinkedIn explains the moderation queue as: allows your group management team to repost or delete group content, as well as review content that has been flagged by your group members. If members within your group feel that a particular post is spammy or worthy of flagging for any reason, it will landing in your moderation inbox.

Moderation Queue

Inappropriate	Promotion	Job

Delete	Clear Flags		Change Permissions ▾

Approved to Post

Requires Moderation

Block & Delete

Take caution using the block and delete features of the moderation queue. It is acceptable to delete something, but using the block and delete option under change permissions will prevent that particular member from potentially having their content approved in any other groups. If any one group manager uses block and delete, some users are experiencing their content always pending moderation in every group. This would be acceptable if the content in question were detrimental to all groups that person participates in, but if the content is merely spammy or off-topic, a simple delete would be far better. If you feel so gracious, send the offender a personal note explaining your decision.

Requests to Join LinkedIn Groups apply for those that have specified users must request and are not automatically approved. Here you'll see all levels of group membership, including the ability to block people from joining the group.

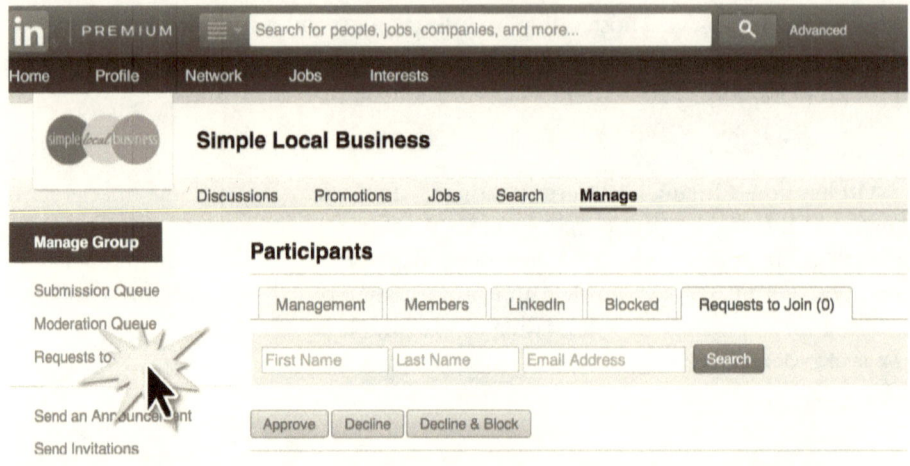

Group Announcements

Once per week group owners can send a group announcement. This can be a great way to draw members back to something you'd like to highlight on your group, or lead them to something that has happened on your own website.

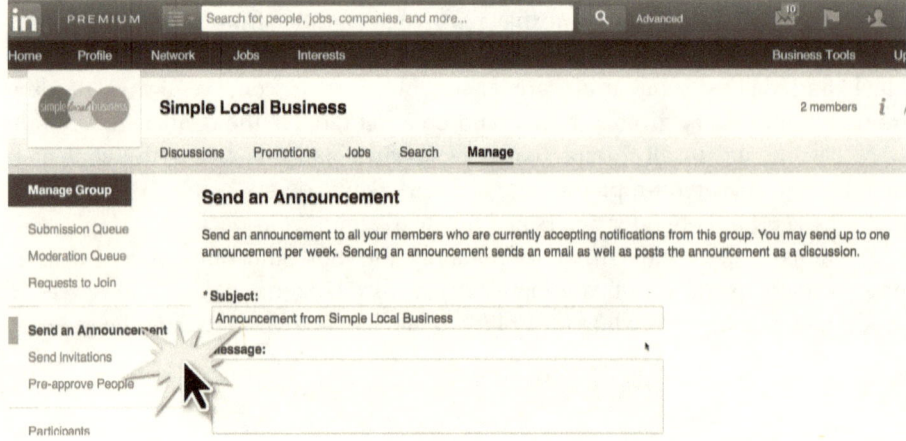

Each announcement can contain up to 200 characters in the title, and 4,000 characters in the body of the message. Remember to put thought into making your title count as these announcements are delivered to group members who have allowed group owners to send them announcements via email.

Group Invitations

Inviting others to your group is important to build community early. As your group grows, inviting people may not be so necessary. You can use the Group Manager dashboard for that, or you can personally email people the link. I prefer to share the link that is specifically available in the bottom left of the manager invite panel rather than the built in invite option because I want to customize the message. Consider other ways that you can share the invite link via your website, blog, or other social channels as well.

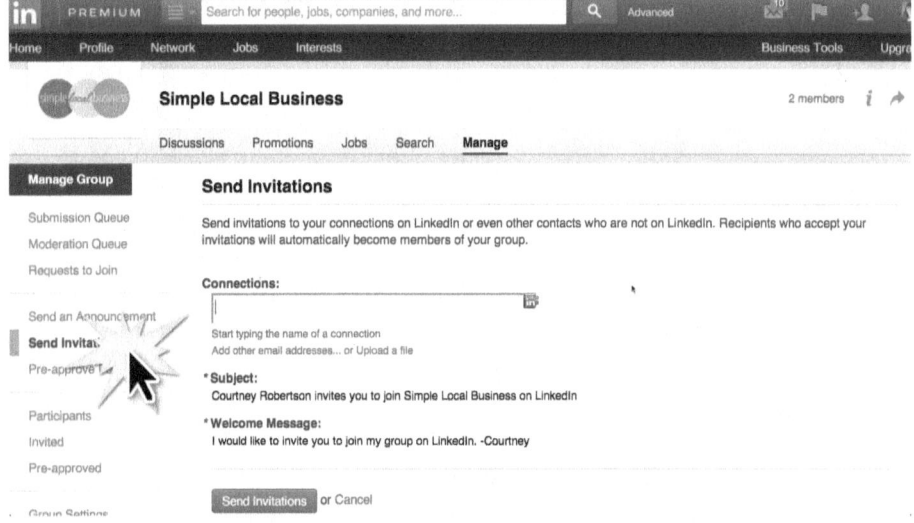

Pre-Approved Group Members

By pre-approving members, you can set your group to require a request to join unless they are on your pre-approved list. You can type their contact name into the connection box or upload a .csv file of people.

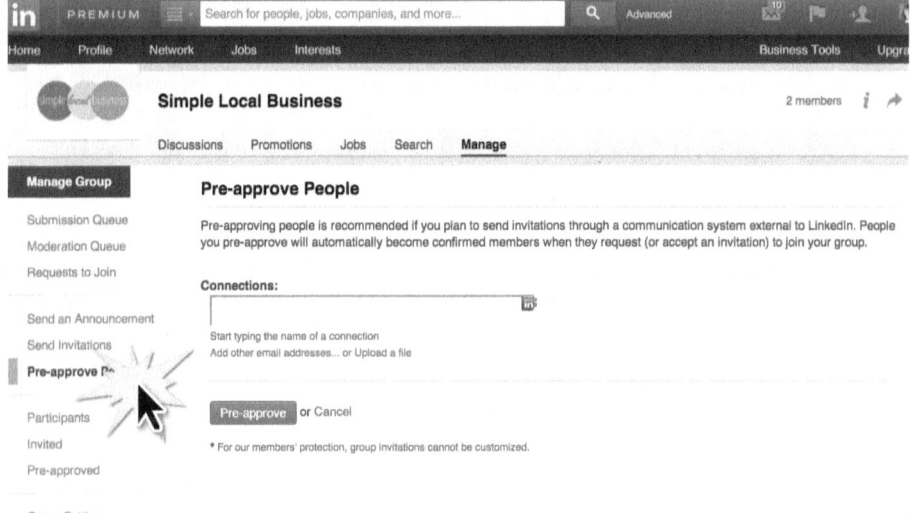

Group Settings

Your group settings allow you to enable and disable many features within your group. You can allow Polls, Promotions, Jobs, and Subgroups from this panel as well as modifying group permissions.

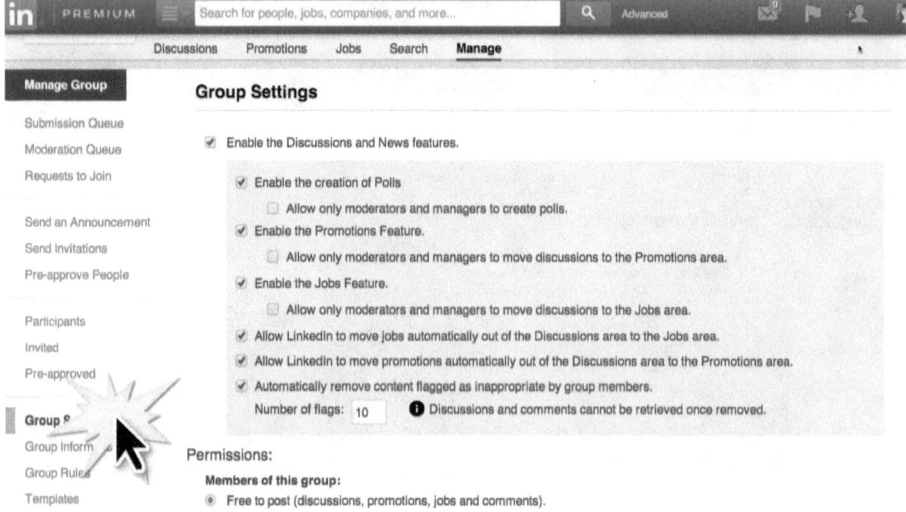

Edit Group Information

If after creating your group you decide to modify the logo or descriptions, go to the group settings area. You'll be presented with the ability to modify all aspects of your group, including 4 times to change the name.

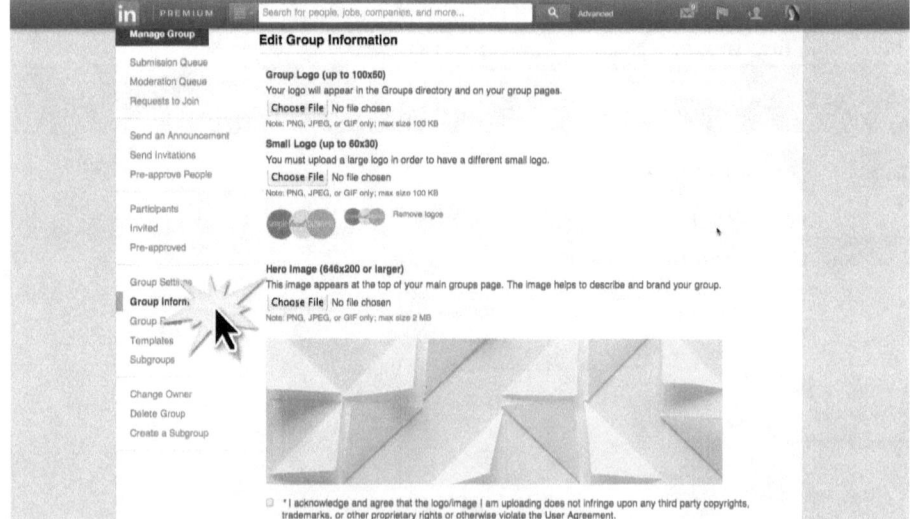

Edit Group Rules

When members are previewing your group, providing rules for the group will ensure that members know your parameters and how to create the most value for all members. Take a peak at a few other group rules before drafting your own.

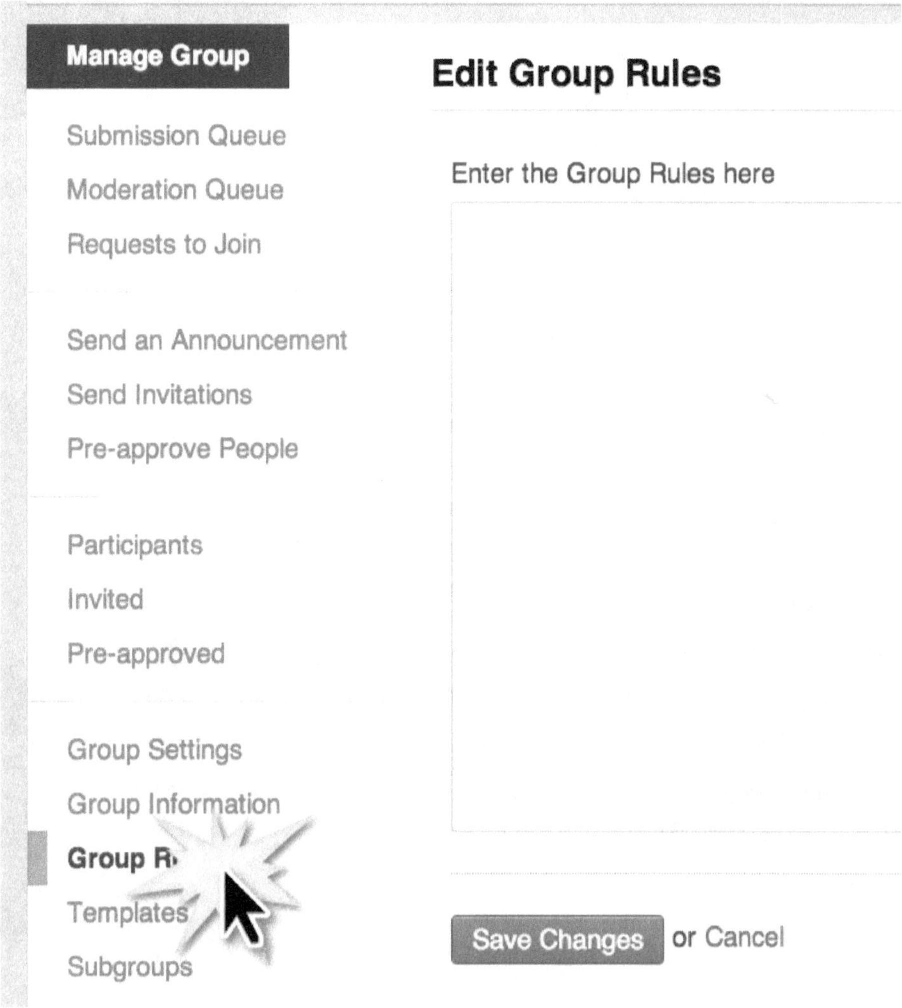

Manage Group

Submission Queue

Moderation Queue

Requests to Join

Send an Announcement

Send Invitations

Pre-approve People

Participants

Invited

Pre-approved

Group Settings

Group Information

Group R

Templates

Subgroups

Edit Group Rules

Enter the Group Rules here

Save Changes or Cancel

Group Message Templates

When members are joining your group or you are deleting them from the community, a few message exchanges will factor in. Draft your message templates to expedite your time managing groups.

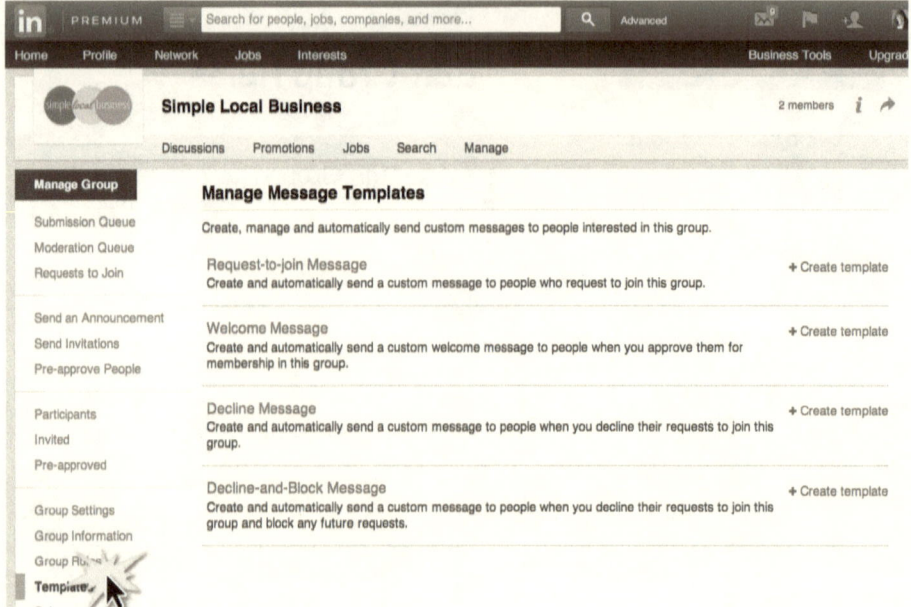

Creating and Managing Subgroups

Subgroups can be a valuable way to further connect your community. You can be a member of 50 or own a total of 20 subgroups. To be a member of a subgroup, the person must be a member of the main group. Ideas for how to implement these include:

- Regionally based
- Job title
- Speciality focus (An accounting group divided into business, tax, personal, etc.)
- Experience level

To create your subgroup, see the bottom left of the manage dashboard, or the subgroup option to manage these.

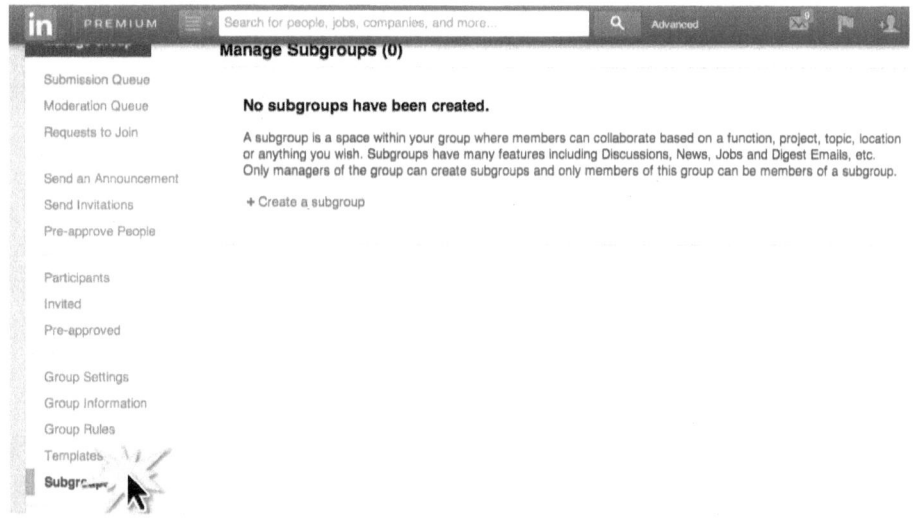

Consider the following tips:
*   A group logo that reflects the main group branding
*   List the subgroups in the group rules
*   Wait until the main group is very active before introducing sub-groups.

See the LinkedIn Group "Jobs" for a listing of subgroups: http://www.linkedin.com/groups/Subgroups-Career-Job-Targeted-Opportunities-1976445.S.111450954

Changing Group Owners and Deleting a Group

Should you need to hand off ownership of a group, LinkedIn does make that possible. Likewise, you can also delete a group.

Change Owner

Delete Group

Organize Your Groups

Before fully developing your strategy for networking via LinkedIn Groups, you may find it highly beneficial to organize the groups that you've joined. While viewing your groups, go to the "reorder" option to organize the order in which you see your list of groups. Go to http://www.linkedin.com/anet?dispSortAnets to sort how you would like your groups to appear.

You can specify how many groups you'd like to see in the "Group" drop navigation menu, as well as shuffle the order of groups around to fit your needs.

Your LinkedIn Groups Strategy

How you use groups to meet your strategy goals is entirely your choice. I've organized the groups that I belong to in the following ways:

- Groups that I own or moderate are first in my order and are visited at least daily
- Roughly 10 groups that I visit one to three times per week are next on my list. I use my daily task lists to remind me every Monday to check in on a few of these, Tuesday has it's own groups I visit, and so on.
- At the bottom of the order of my groups are those that I joined solely to expand my network and seldom vist
- In the middle are those groups that I visit more often via my mobile devices as it provides a clean layout. I see these less often, but occasionally contribute.

While visiting the groups that I am a member of, I have a few points that I look for:

- First, read any recent updates by others. Comment on their activity.
- Occasionally, welcome new members by commenting on their contributions.
- Ask a specific group a question that I believe they would be experts about.
- Share significant news
- Promote myself or anything that benefits me sparingly

If you are the owner of a group, a few tips for engagement include:

- Selecting a weekly or daily theme or topic. Create a discussion with this.
- Pose questions to the group
- Share related articles
- Discuss current news in the related industry
- Use Polls to foster engagement
- Ask members for feedback

JOBS

LinkedIn is a great service for jobseekers and those looking to hire. However, our focus in Simple Local Business and this book is primarily on small business owners and not on job seekers. As such, this will be a brief overview, but there are plenty of additional resources for job seekers. If you are a job seeker, you may choose to list your company as "Open to New Opportunities".

Job Overview

LinkedIn has long been known as a network to join when you are seeking a job. Visit the Jobs section.

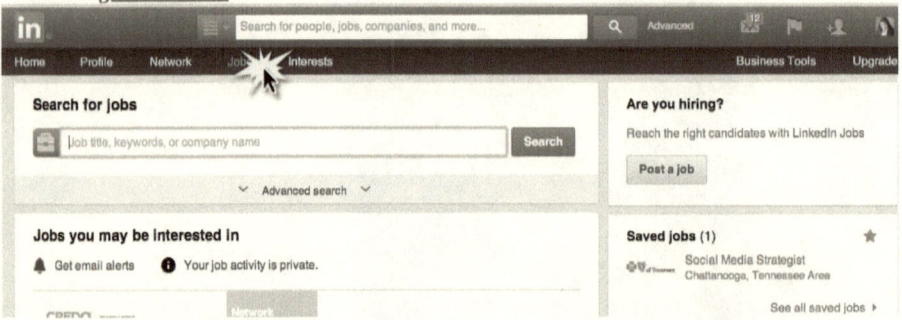

On the sidebar you'll notice a quick shortcut to posting a job, seeing your saved searches, and viewing your network connection statistics.

Saved jobs (1)

 Social Media Strategist
Chattanooga, Tennessee Area

See all saved jobs ▸

Saved searches (2)

- web developer 50 mi (80 km)
  15 new results

- social media 100 mi (160 km)
  73 new results

See all saved searches ▸

Applied Jobs

Review your past job applications here.

See all applied jobs ▸

Job Seeker Toolkit

100% Your profile is 100% complete. Keep your profile up to date.

2169 You have 2,169 connections. Add connections to build your network.

34 You are following 34 companies. Follow companies that interest you.

Jobs You May Be Interested In

Based on the content of your completed profile, you will be presented with jobs that may be of interest to you. Note that by default, no one can see what job openings you are viewing or searching for.

You can receive email alerts of LinkedIn's suggested job based upon the frequency that you specify. See the alert prompt.

Email Alert Settings

Receive email alerts for Jobs You May Be Interested In:

○ Daily

● Weekly

○ No email alerts

Save or Cancel

Discover Jobs In Your Network

Rather than suggestions based upon your profile information, LinkedIn also has suggestions based upon the people in your network. This is where practicing open networking is incredibly valuable. Having many connections can become most useful when searching for jobs.

Discover jobs in your network

Reach out to your connections for a referral

LinkedIn Careers
417 jobs

Kelly Services Careers
93 jobs

Expedia Careers
522 jobs

Viewing these job positions will take you to the company page's career tab, as seen with a suggested network career at Google.

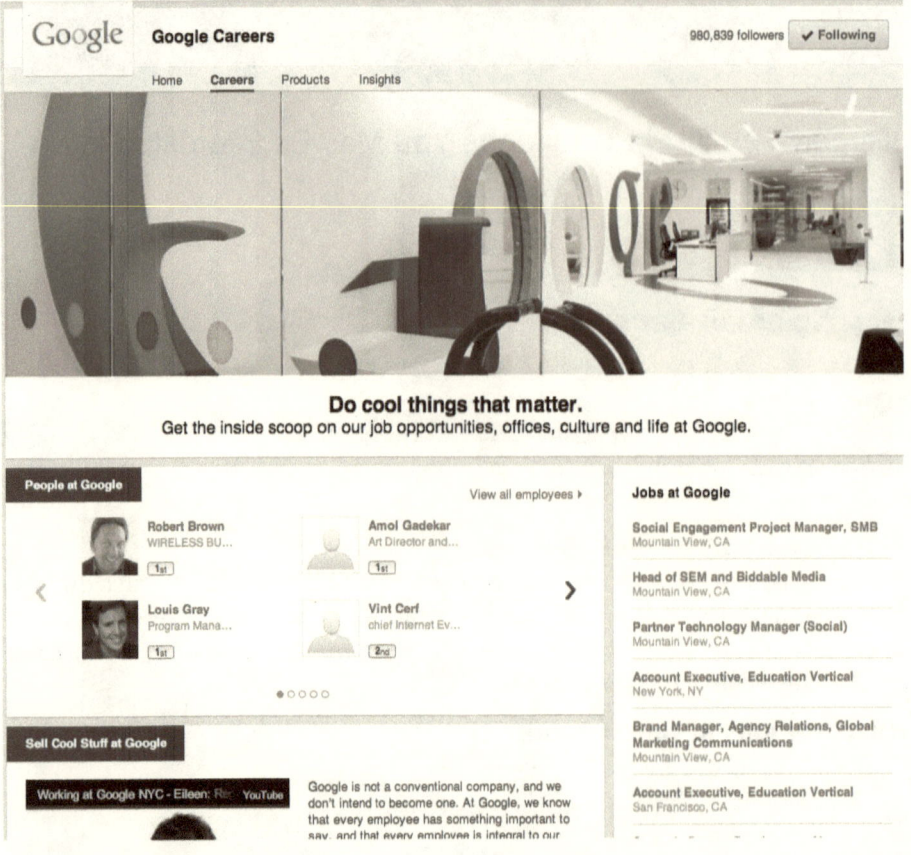

Viewing Job Postings

As you review job postings, you'll see the basic job description and company location. It is good, even if not job hunting, to look at the layout of this section in the event you post a job to hire for your company. See the job listings as if you were the job seeker. Notice anything that compels you and remember that if you post a job.

Director, Digital Marketing Strategy & Insights

Harte-Hanks, Inc. - Yardley, PA (Greater Philadelphia Area)

Job Description

Provide digital marketing strategy for existing agency clients and prospects, including email marketing, Web sites, social media and mobile marketing. Provide insight and direction on data derived from marketing, social media, mobile and Web data. Support other team members in digital media strategy and insights.

Digital Marketing Strategy & Insights Primary Functions

- Provide digital marketing campaign strategy, as an integrated component of campaigns and as stand-alone campaign
- Provide direction on digital marketing solution development, including Web sites, applications, mobile and social network asset
- Provide email marketing campaign strategy as an integrated or stand alone campaign.
- Collaborate with strategic resources on social media and digital marketing campaigns
- Create and/or collaborate on social and digital media insights
- Provide social and digital media reporting recommendations
- Collaborate with strategic and analytic resources
- Create social and digital marketing measurement plans

Goals and Expectations

Below you'll find further company information along with any further details and the ability to apply for the job.

Company Description

The Agency Inside Harte-Hanks is a creatively inspired, data-obsessed relationship marketing agency focused on building value through continuous relevant customer experiences. The Agency Inside Harte-Hanks was founded in 1983 (as DiMark). The expertise we began building in those early years has grown exponentially, as we have helped our clients navigate the many changes in the relationship marketing landscape over the years. We were acquired by Harte-Hanks Corporation in 1996 and from that time we evolved from Harte-Hanks Direct into the agency we are today.

Additional Information

Posted:	March 14, 2013
Type:	Full-time
Experience:	Mid-Senior level
Functions:	Strategy/Planning
Industries:	Marketing and Advertising
Job ID:	5119373

> **Apply Now**

🔥 On Fire!
74 people have applied

Note that you can see what other people who have viewed this job have also viewed. This could be a great way to discover options you previously hadn't found in search results.

People Who Viewed This Job Also Viewed

- Director of Digital Marketing Strategy at **Wolters Kluwer**
- Director of Digital Marketing + Content Strategy at **Ten Adams**
- Director of Marketing at **IMS Health**
- Corporate Marketing Manager at **PREIT**
- VP of Relationship Development at **Harte-Hanks, Inc.**
- Director, Marketing Communications at **IMS Health**
- Director of Digital Marketing -NYC at **Kaplan Inc.**
- Director of Digital Marketing at **The Washington Post**

On the top right, you can apply for a job. You're also able to see how many others have applied for this position and to save the job for viewing later.

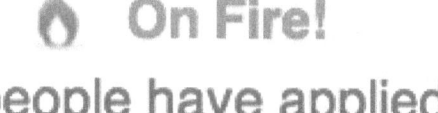

Apply Now

🔥 On Fire!

74 people have applied

💾 Save job | **View saved jobs »**

📠 Share job [in] [f] [tw]

Follow company

When you view the saved jobs, you can also viewed job applications and saved searches.

You can see who posted the job and who to contact. You will see how you are connected to this listing and send an InMail if that fits into your LinkedIn plan.

Posted By

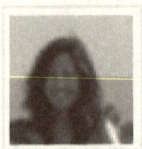

Maggie Dietrich (2nd)
Sr. Talent Acquisition Partner
Send InMail

1 of your connections can refer you to Maggie:

Michael Cuff (1st)
Director, Client Services Career
Concepts Incorporated
Request Introduction to Maggie

If you choose to apply for a job, you will be able to include your profile, compose a cover letter, and upload a resume.

Director, Digital Marketing Strategy & Insights
Harte-Hanks, Inc. - Greater Philadelphia Area

Courtney Robertson
Digital Marketing Strategist, Public Speaker, Author,
Owner, Trainer at Simple Local Business (Sole
Proprietorship)
Harrisburg, Pennsylvania Area

Your profile will be included with your application. **Update »**

Experience: Digital Marketing Strategist, Public Speaker,
Author, Owner, Trainer at Simple Local
Business

Social Media Strategist, Internet Marketing
Consultant, Project Manager at Timao
Multimedia

Social Media, Local SEO, and Mobile
Marketing Strategist at Social Mobile Local
Marketing Pros

See all...

Education: Shippensburg University of Pennsylvania

Bloomsburg University of Pennsylvania

See all...

* Email: courtney@courtneyengle.com ⬍

Add email addresses to your account

* Telephone:

Cover Letter: Add cover letter

Resume: Choose File No file chosen

Formats: MS Word, PDF, Text, HTML (200K maximum)

✓ **Follow Harte-Hanks, Inc.** to stay up-to-date on the
latest news and career opportunities

This won't be shared with your network

Submit or Cancel

* Required Field

Search for a Job

When you search for a job, you can add in several keywords that fit your industry. Sort based upon your needs and narrow down your results by region.

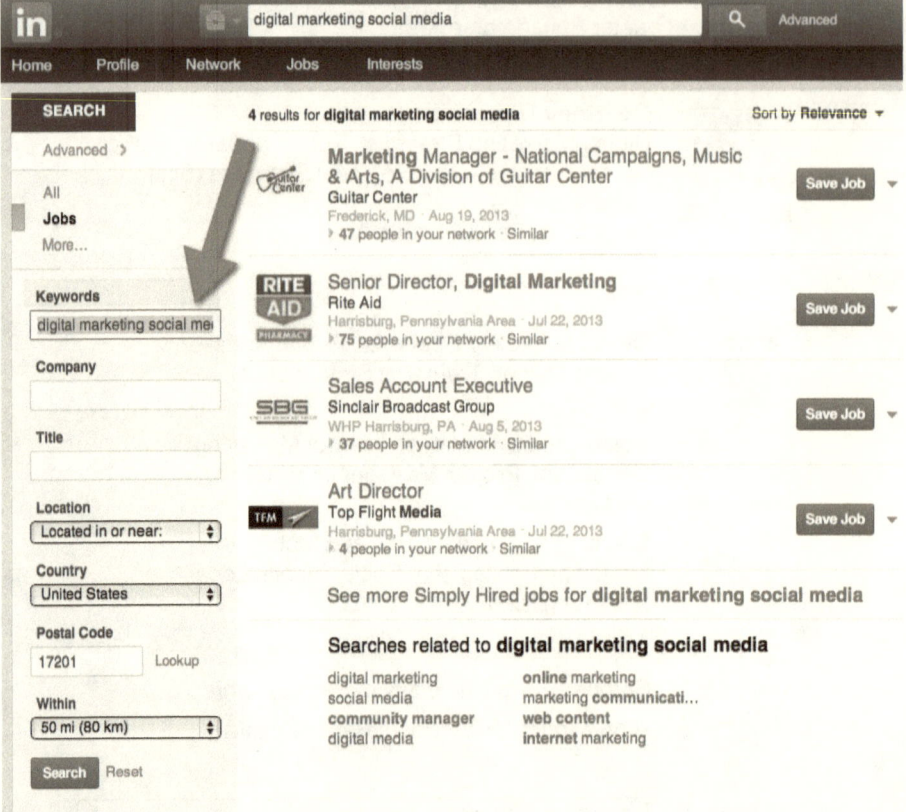

Refine your search based upon a few criteria, like what location and how recently the job was posted.

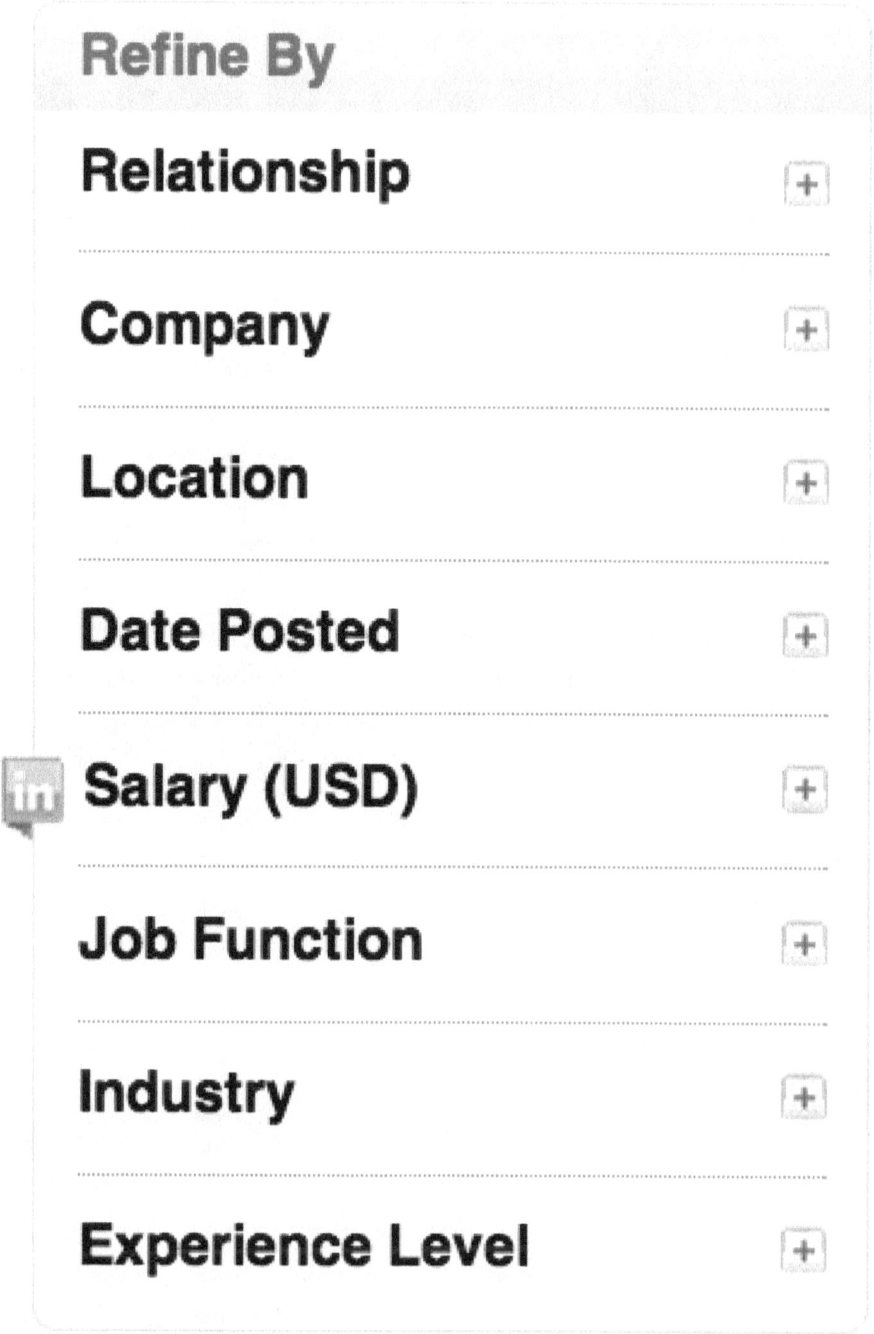

Refine By

Relationship `+`

Company `+`

Location `+`

Date Posted `+`

Salary (USD) `+`

Job Function `+`

Industry `+`

Experience Level `+`

Save your job searches for viewing later.

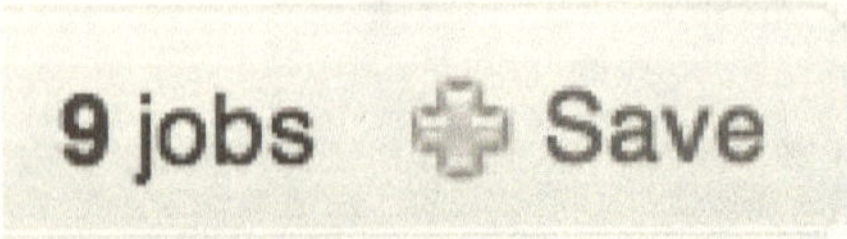

9 jobs 🔲 Save

Be sure to save the search name with a specific title for later reference.

Save This Job Search

Search Name: digital marketing social media

Send Email Alert: Weekly ⬍

Save or Cancel

Advanced Search

Using the Advanced Job Search option, you can specify parameters or requirements for your results. By setting salary caps, locations, industries, and more, you will be able to find further details about the jobs posted on LinkedIn.

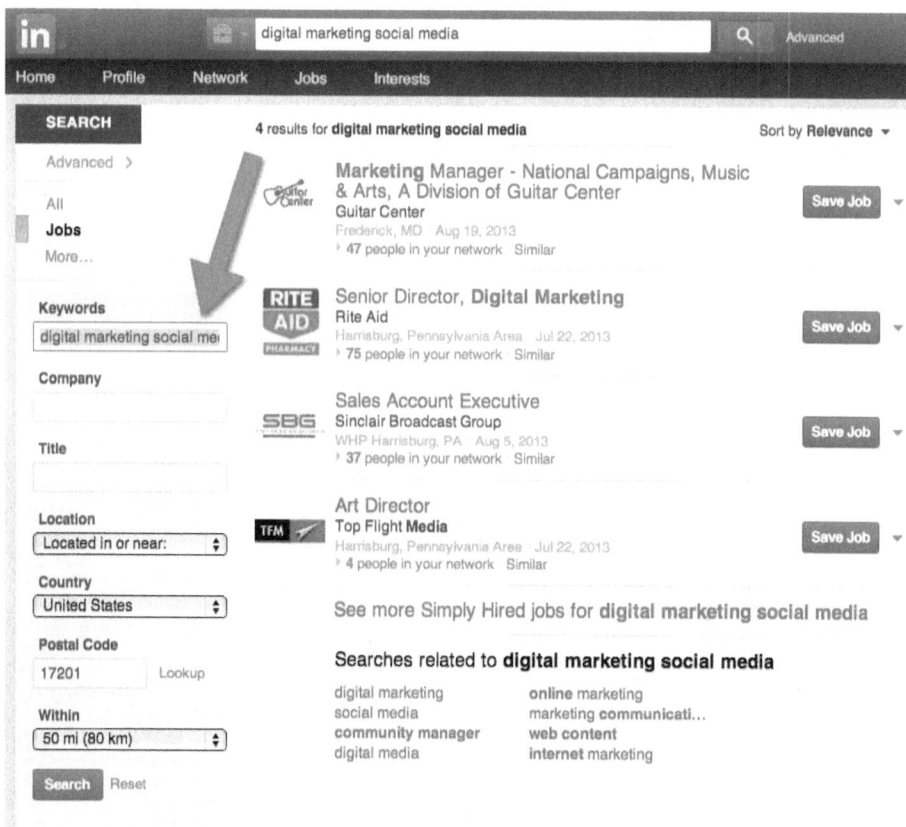

in   digital marketing social media   🔍 Advanced

Home   Profile   Network   Jobs   Interests

SEARCH

Advanced >

All
Jobs
More...

Keywords

digital marketing social mer

Company

Title

Location

Located in or near: ⬍

Country

United States ⬍

Postal Code

17201   Lookup

Within

50 mi (80 km) ⬍

Search   Reset

4 results for **digital marketing social media**   Sort by **Relevance** ▾

Marketing Manager - National Campaigns, Music & Arts, A Division of Guitar Center
Guitar Center
Frederick, MD · Aug 19, 2013
› **47** people in your network · Similar   Save Job ▾

Senior Director, Digital Marketing
Rite Aid
Harrisburg, Pennsylvania Area · Jul 22, 2013
› **75** people in your network · Similar   Save Job ▾

Sales Account Executive
Sinclair Broadcast Group
WHP Harrisburg, PA · Aug 5, 2013
› **37** people in your network · Similar   Save Job ▾

Art Director
Top Flight **Media**
Harrisburg, Pennsylvania Area · Jul 22, 2013
› **4** people in your network · Similar   Save Job ▾

See more Simply Hired jobs for **digital marketing social media**

Searches related to digital marketing social media

digital marketing   **online** marketing
social media   marketing **communicati...**
community manager   **web content**
digital media   **internet** marketing

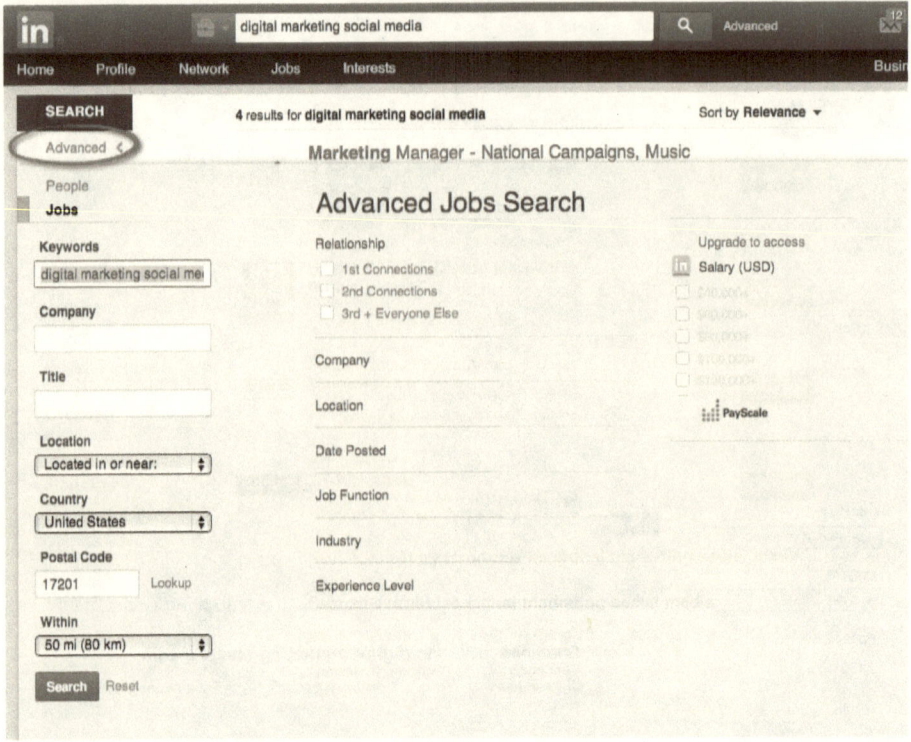

If you are a job seeker, you may want to review the additional options in the Job Seeker Premium account options, which will place a yellow briefcase symbol on your profile and open additional job seeker opportunities. Options are also available for Recruiters and Sales Professionals.

Why use Job Search When You Aren't Looking for a Job

As you are most likely a business owner, you aren't likely to be looking for a job. However, this can be instead a great way to find specific people within companies that you may want to do business with. If you were searching for a point of contact at a company that would oversee a specific department, try using the job search to discover them. You would not be limited in this way to seeing only a few degrees of separation in your existing network of connections, but be able to find specific people and their job title within companies this way. The key is to consider what the point-of-contact you seek would be overseeing in hiring and job postings. Get creative with the job search tool even if you are not seeking employment.

Post a Job

Posting a job is far more likely to be of interest to small business owners than how to get hired. It will cost you a variable rate to post your job. The cost of job listings is dependent upon your region. In my area of Harrisburg, PA, a job listing starts at $195 for a 30 day listing. In more urban areas it can start at $250 or more. View the Post a Job area within Jobs.

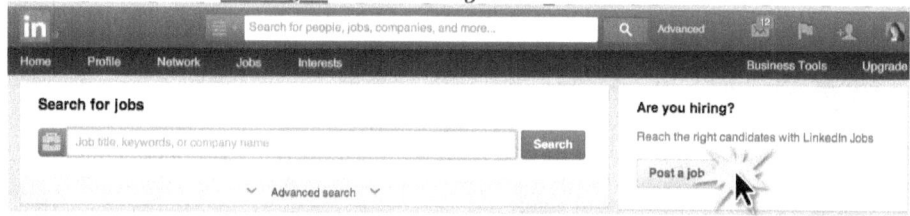

As you complete your job listing, the information will also integrate to the jobs tab on your company profile.

Before writing your listing, take a look at other job listings. This will help you know what phrases and layout options others in your market are using. Write the job titles and descriptions based upon what terms your ideal applicants will be using when searching for you. Keep your desired skills and strengths concise. Applicants will be quickly reading your listing, and focusing their attention only on what is essential will help the application process progress to the interviews where more details can be discussed. Give respondents a brief idea of the steps in your recruiting process so they know where they stand and stay engaged.

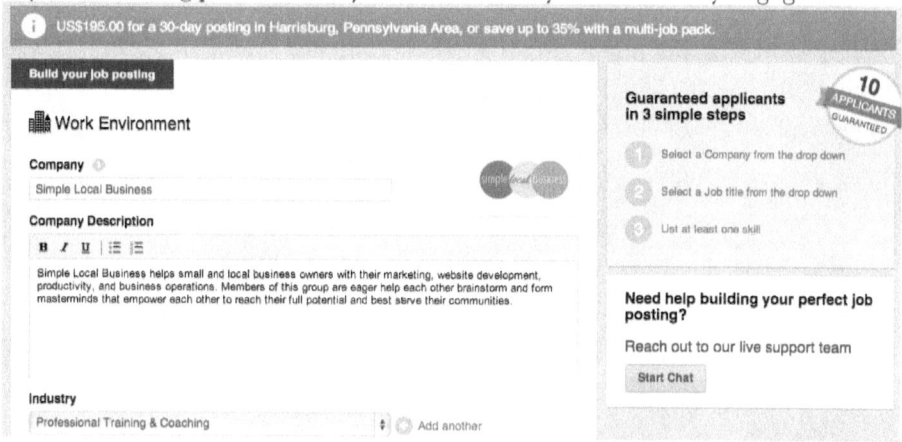

If you are aggressively looking to fill a job position, consider the Talent Finder plan. This plan is often used by hiring agencies and larger companies, but may be valuable for quickly finding the right person for the job. With it, you can take the initiative to request those not in your network to apply for the position. It also allows you to ask potential references about the applicants.

Announce Your Job Post

Once you've created your job post, get the most out of it. Share it on your LinkedIn status update, on your other social media accounts, from your website, and in your email newsletters. Hang a sign in your store and let your network of connections know that you are hiring.

Share Jobs on Your Website

If you've listed a job on LinkedIn, you can make it easy for people browsing your website to apply for it. Visit here https://developer.linkedin.com/plugins#apply to get some code to copy/paste to the appropriate page on your website.

Apply with LinkedIn

Make it easy for candidates to apply for your jobs using their LinkedIn profiles.

With Apply with LinkedIn, you can start accepting job applications with a few lines of code. Customize the interface with your company logo and color and add up to three custom yes or no questions. You can also integrate with your Applicant Tracking System. Add Apply with LinkedIn to jobs on your site to attract top talent today.

Get it   Learn More

If you'd like to list multiple jobs that your company offers, you can do that as well at https://developer.linkedin.com/plugins#jymbii

Jobs You May Be Interested In

Boost site engagement with personalized job listings.

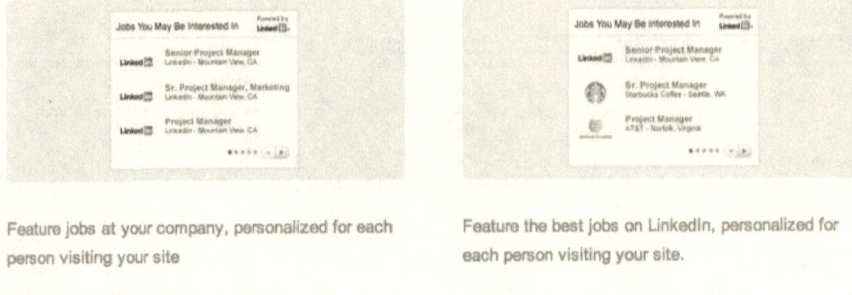

Feature jobs at your company, personalized for each person visiting your site

Feature the best jobs on LinkedIn, personalized for each person visiting your site.

Get it   Get it

LinkedIn Jobs

While many people on LinkedIn are not actively seeking a job, it is estimated that about 60% of people on LinkedIn are open to new employment opportunities when presented with a good fit. Whether you use jobs to find employment, make a new connection with a key person at a company you'd like to connect with, or to hire people the right person for your business, LinkedIn jobs are worth your time. LinkedIn has been built up by job seekers and those hiring, yet is able to do much more for small business owners. Don't overlook what you may find by reviewing the jobs section.

COMPANY PAGES

LinkedIn Company Pages are the place your business needs to be represented. Not only can company updates display in the news stream on followers main LinkedIn dashboard, but the profile stands out well in search results, can generate leads, and is a great way to continue connecting with followers. In addition, job seekers can look to your Company Page to discover if your business has any positions available.

LinkedIn Company Pages

To view LinkedIn Company Pages, navigate to Interest, Company Pages.

Companies Home

When you view the Companies Home tab, you'll be quickly presented with a search box. This is a quick way to start a search, though the same can be done under the "search companies" tab as well.

Search for Companies

| | **Search** |

Company Name, Keywords, or Industry

What Companies Should You Follow?

You can follow up to 1,000 Company Pages on LinkedIn, but what companies should you follow?

- Your own
- Businesses that provide you services
- Businesses that you network with
- Competition
- Organizations within your community (chambers of commerce) or that you are a paying member of
- Stellar business pages (Hubspot)
- Simple Local Business

Followed Company Updates

Once you've followed a few companies, you'll be able to see the updates that each of these companies share.

Followed Company Updates

 Salesforce Marketing Cloud A look at takeaways from the NASA Mars Rover social media campaign. Winners of the SXSWI "Best Social Media Campaign" award. http://mrkt.rs/ZEYP8m

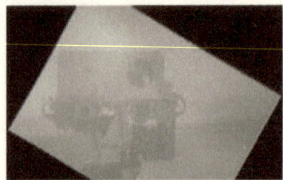 5 Tips to Create Social Media Campaigns That Aren't Boring -...
salesforcemarketingcloud.com
A few Takeaways from NASA's Curiosity Rover social media campaign. Winners of the SXSWi Best social media campaign award for 2013.

Like · Comment · Share · 40 minutes ago

 LinkedIn When sales people start Social Selling they go to Linkedin: http://slidesha.re/WRZrZM

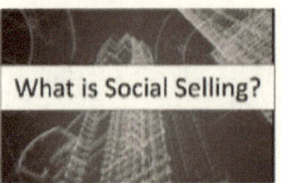 What is social selling
slideshare.net
Social Selling is the use of social networks to find and engage with decision makers. The BEST social network to empower social selling is LinkedIn.

Like (9) · Comment · Share · 1 hour ago

These updates can also be viewed in your main LinkedIn dashboard. By default, when a person follows a company, that will be displayed to their connections in LinkedIn. This can be disabled in settings, or hidden in the updates area.

_____ _____ is now following:

cloudera ⬛⬛⬛ CÍTR|X ▲ IRON MOUNTAIN

Cloudera

Cloudera is the leader in Apache Hadoop-based software and services and a powerful new data platform that enables enterprises and organizations to loo data — structured as well as unstructured — and ask bigger questions for...
San Francisco Bay Area, 201-500 Employees

View company · 2 minutes ago

_____ _____ is now following:

Cigniti ▷ISYS

Cigniti Inc

Cigniti is a pure play, Independent Software Testing Services Company and i listed. Over the last 14 years Cigniti has worked with leading ISVs and Enter organisations to deliver quality software using proprietary PREDICT QUALIT
Dallas/Fort Worth Area, 501-1000 Employees

View company · 1 hour ago

Companies ▾

Top

Recent

All Updates

Connections

Profiles

Shares

Groups

Companies

New

Jobs

Your Updates

Hidden (1) »

Customize »

RSS »

Companies You Might Want to Follow

Not only will LinkedIn suggest companies for you to follow on the Companies Home tab, but also on Following tab. LinkedIn looks at the other companies you are following and the content in your personal profile to suggest these results. You'll be able to see more than just these.

Companies You May Want to Follow

  2020S◎CIAL

Feedback I See more »

Your Company Page

If you've created your own Company Page or listed yourself as an employee, you'll be able to see a preview of your company.

 # Simple Local Business

Simple Local Business helps small and local business owners with their marketing, website development, productivity, and business operations. Members of this group are eager help each other ...
More »

HQ:	Harrisburg, Pennsylvania Area
Industry:	Professional Training & Coaching
Type:	Sole Proprietorship
Status:	Operating
Size:	Myself Only
Founded:	2013
Website:	http://simplelocalbusines...

Edit info I See company page »

Search Companies

When you visit "Search Companies" you'll be presented with a listing of results. These results can be narrowed down to what is more relevant to you.

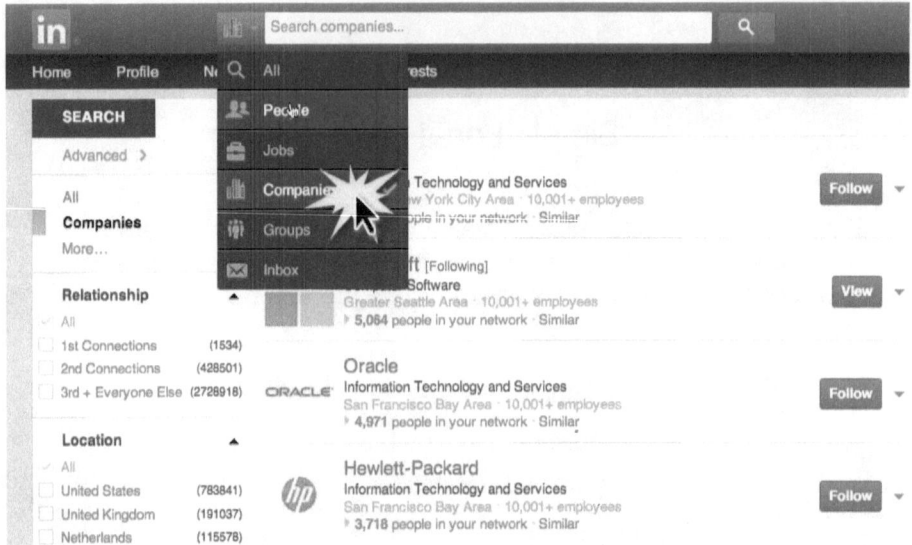

Search

On the top search box, search for a company by name or use a keyword to find companies offering what you seek. Use the drop option to the left of the search box to filter specifically to companies.

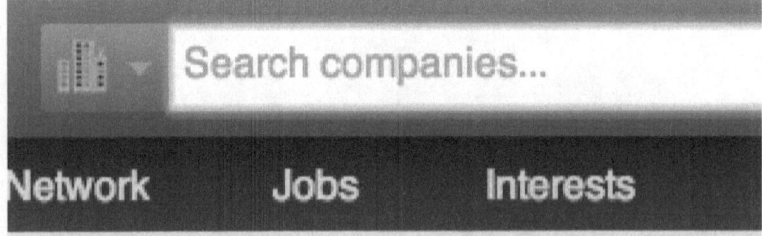

Refine By

The results you get by searching may not be ideal. Narrow down your results by selecting filters. This could be used to find an accountant that services your region, locate companies within your city that are hiring, and learn what companies in your industry have the largest number of followers.

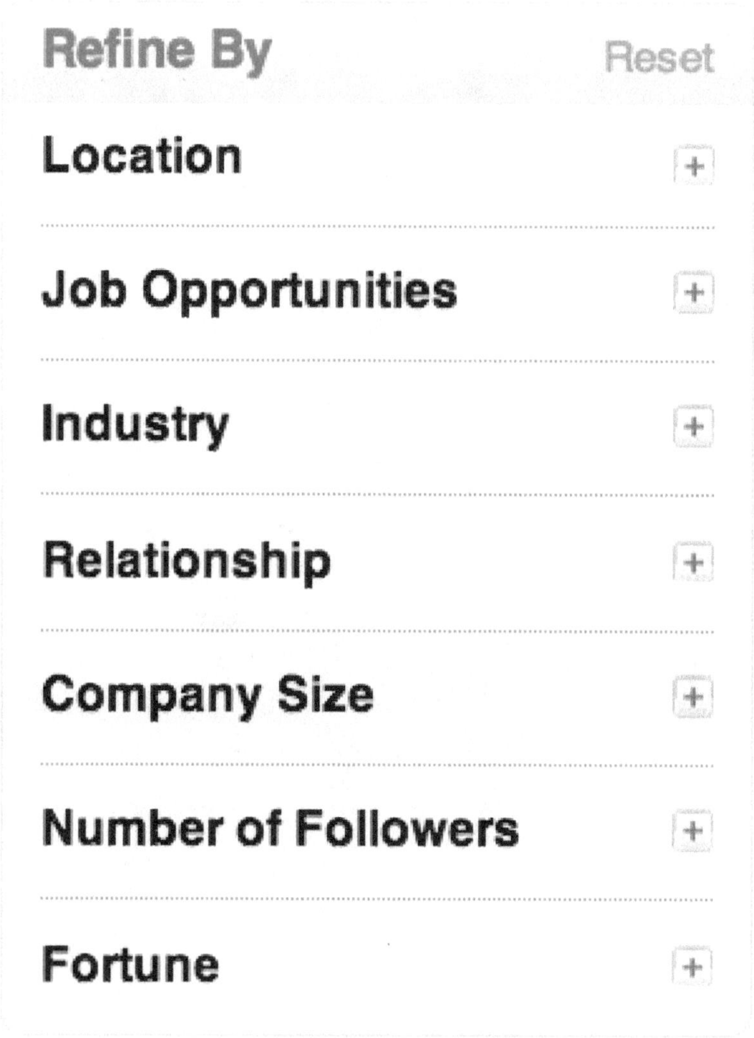

Refine By

Reset

Location `+`

Job Opportunities `+`

Industry `+`

Relationship `+`

Company Size `+`

Number of Followers `+`

Fortune `+`

Sort By

To have even more control of your search results than just refining them, you can sort the information. If you want an accountant in your town that is a part of a large company, sorting by company size can narrow down these results.

Following

In the following tab, you can see a list of the companies that you have followed, as well as suggestions.

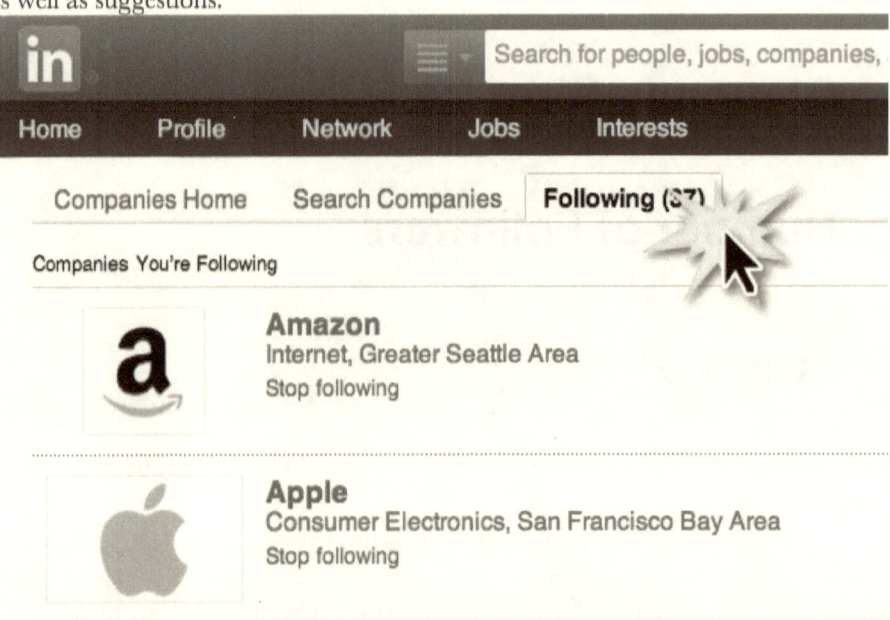

Companies You're Following

Note that you can stop following a company from this list, or click to view that specific company page.

Companies You Might Want to Follow

Again, suggested companies are viewable.

Viewing Company Pages   113

When you view a company page, you'll get an overview of that specific company. Hubspot's company page is a great example that generates considerable leads for their business.

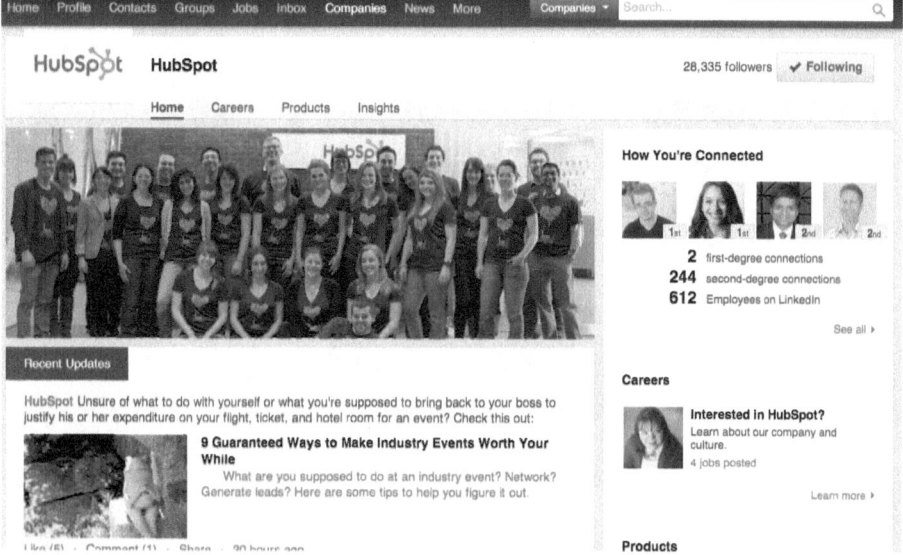

Logo & Following

You'll notice when viewing a company page that you can see a logo, follow or unfollow the page, view how many others are following the page, and a header image.

If you click on the number of followers, you'll see a list of those following this company page that have not made that information private.

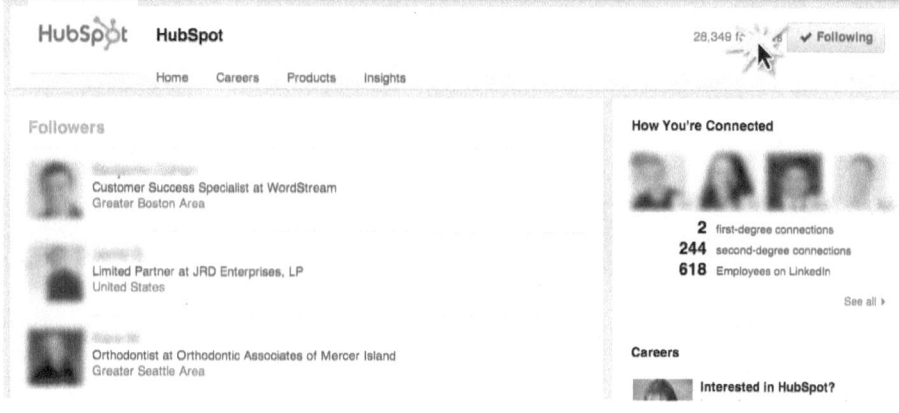

Recent Updates

From the overview of a company page, you'll see the recent updates that company has listed. This can be a status update as text, a link to an article, or a file that can be attached (like a graphic or pdf). Followers can like, comment, and share that update. This places the company page's update in front of all their followers connections.

When you follow a company, take part in interacting on their updates.

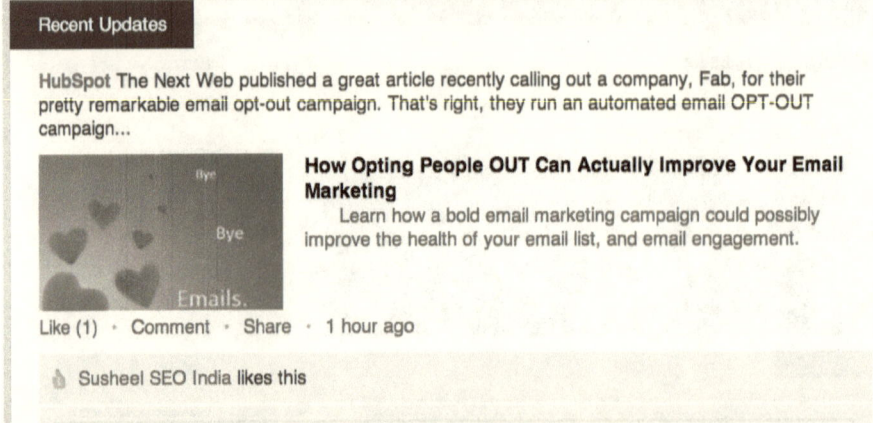

About

At the bottom of the company page, you'll see the about information. This is a great place to get an overview of this company and learn quick stats about the size and location of the company.

About HubSpot

Welcome to HubSpot's home on LinkedIn! Follow us for regular updates about marketing tips, blog articles, free webinars and more. We pride ourselves for being friendly and helpful.

Also, check out our PRODUCTS TAB to see some of our most popular free webinars.

So ... What is HubSpot?

HubSpot is an inbound marketing software company that helps businesses transform their marketing from outbound (cold calls, email spam, trade shows, tv ads, etc) lead generation to inbound lead generation enabling them to "get found" by more potential customers in the natural course of the way they shop and learn.

Since founding in 2006 at MIT, HubSpot has raised four rounds of venture capital from Tier A investors, Matrix, General Catalyst, Scale Ventures, Sequoia Capital, Google Ventures, and Salesforce.com totaling $65 million. The company has over 7,500 paying customers. HubSpot has several free tools that you may already be familiar with including Website Grader and Twitter Grader.

HubSpot's blog (http://blog.hubspot.com) is one of the top 5 marketing blogs, the company has won over 50 marketing awards, and HubSpot has been featured in the Wall Street Journal, the New York Times, TechCrunch, ReadWriteWeb, Mashable, and a number of TV news programs.

Specialties
inbound marketing, marketing, internet marketing, online marketing, web marketing, software, blogging, SEO, marketing automation, social media, email marketing, analytics

Headquarters	Website	Industry
25 First Street 2nd Floor Cambridge, MA 02141 United States	http://www.HubSpot.com	Internet
	Type	**Company Size**
	Privately Held	201-500 employees
	Founded	
	2006	

How You're Connected

As you view the company page, you can see how you are connected with any of the employees of that company that have listed their position on their personal profile. If you'd like to see the full list of all employees, including their job titles, click "see all".

How You're Connected

2 first-degree connections

244 second-degree connections

612 Employees on LinkedIn

Featured Groups

On the sidebar of the company Home tab, you'll see "Featured Groups". These are groups that are operated and owned by the company. These groups may be specific to employees or members of the organization, or can just be groups that the company operates. This is a great way to discover groups that you might want to join.

People Also Viewed

You may gain some insight by seeing what other companies people who've viewed this company have also viewed. I don't find the results to be too precise but do find a few good suggestions here.

People Also Viewed

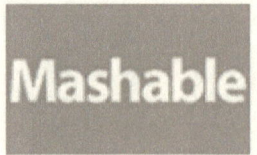

More insights ▶

Career

If you are job seeking or want to discover which person at a company is in a specific department, the Careers tab of a company page is the best way to discover this. Also here you can see a custom header graphic that describes the career page, view all employees, read the "About" section of the company, see recent updates, and discover jobs at that particular company.

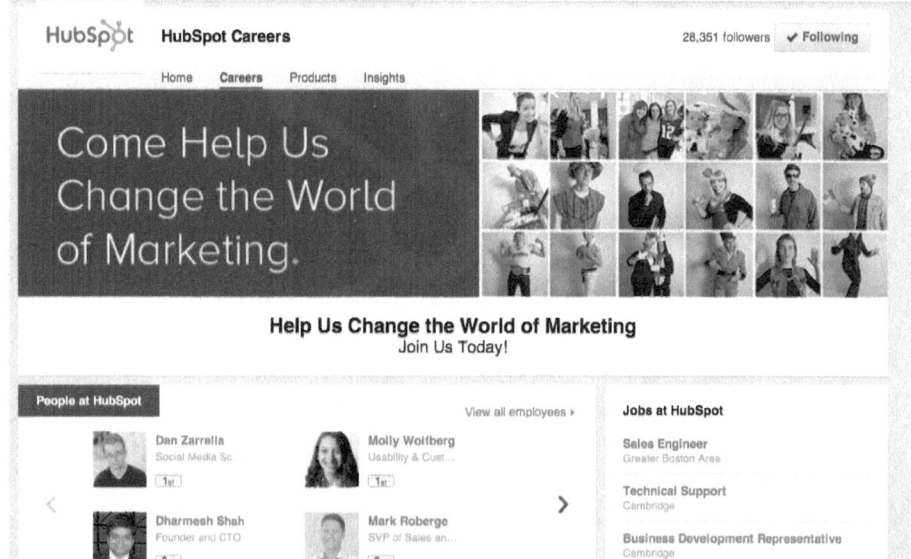

Products

The Products tab within Company Pages is a way to see what products or services this company has to offer. You'll see that the top of the page has a carousel of current products. This page can display 10 of the products listed, though more are available by selecting "next" at the bottom of the page. On each of these products or services, you can recommend or share. On the right side, you'll see recommendations that people have written about each specific product.

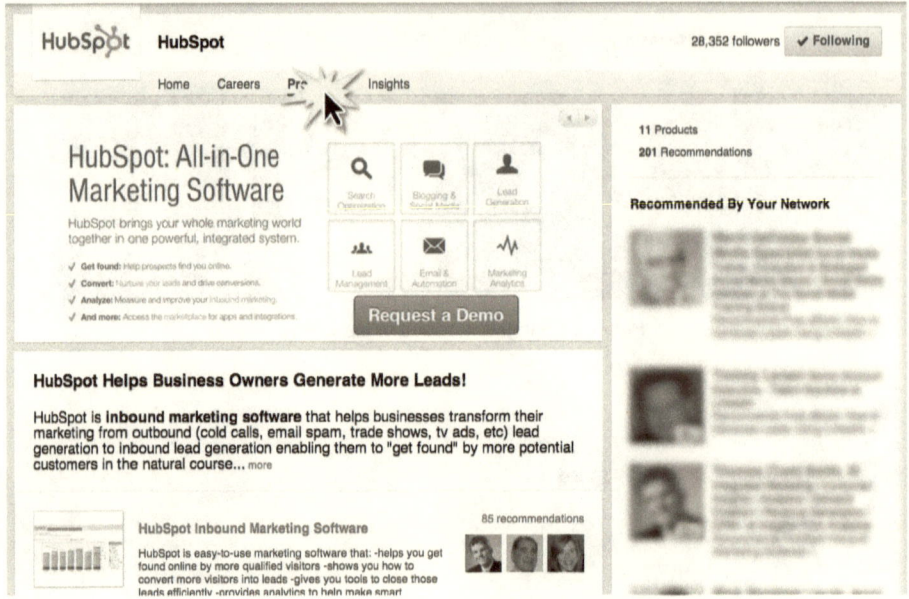

On the right side, you'll see specific promotions that the company has created related to their products.

Grab These Templates for Free:

These HTML templates come in seven packs, each catering to different marketing messages with five separate layouts:

Lead Nurturing Email
Letterhead Email
Landing Page with Offer
Blog Newsletter
Digital Magazine Newsletter

Product Page

Each product on the Products tab has a unique page within the company page. Click on the title to view the full information. You can find who at the company to contact about specific products, visit the company's website, read and write your own recommendations, and possibly view a video related to the product.

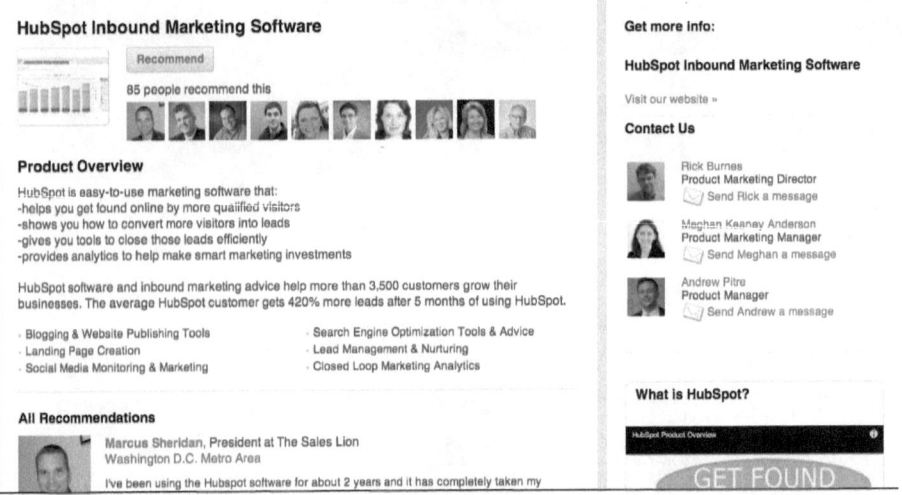

Insights

The Insights tab within a Company's Page can provide valuable insight. You can quickly learn which employees have been promoted or switched job titles, are now former employees, and again see what other companies viewers of this company have also viewed. On the right side you can discover what companies employees have worked at previously, as well as what skills and experience top skills & expertise that members of this company have.

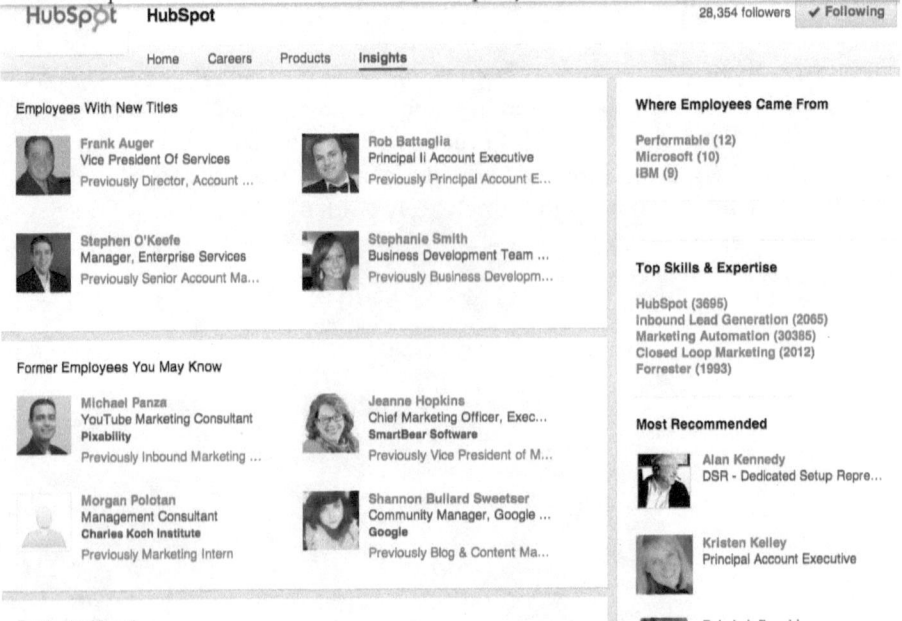

Creating a Company Page

To list your own company page, first do a search to be sure your company isn't listed already. After finding that you are not already listed, add your company from the company page.

Company Overview

Add a Company

Provide your company information. You will need to have an email at your company's domain name. To prevent spam, LinkedIn will not permit company pages to be created via Gmail, AOL, or other free email providers. If you need to add your company email, visit your profile settings.

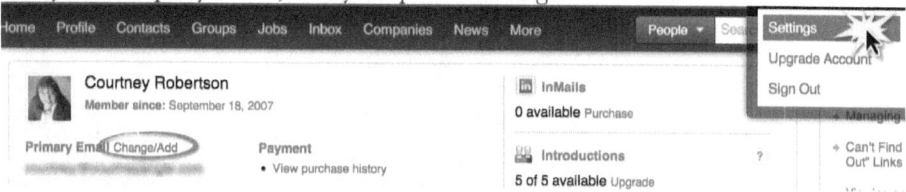

Proceed with adding your company.

Add a Company

Company Pages offer public information about each company on LinkedIn. To add a Company Page, please enter the company name and your email address at this company. Only current employees are eligible to create a Company Page.

Company name:

Your email address at company:

☐ I verify that I am the official representative of this company and have the right to act on behalf of my company in the creation of this page.

Continue or Cancel

Once your page is created, it's time to fill in all the information that you possibly can. Remember that this information should be discoverable by those seeking what you offer. Think like your ideal clients and connections. What would they search for that would bring them to your page? Use those words when describing your company.

If you need ever need to edit these changes, see the top right "Edit" drop menu.

Add product or service

View follower insights

View page insights

Add Jobs

Promote this page with LinkedIn Ads

Simply select the word "Edit" to modify the general information about your company.

Include the name of your company as people would generally refer to it as. Omit details like Inc., LLC or acronyms unless that is the common name. You have 2,000 characters to use, and these are a great place to include your keywords. Like on your profile use special characters, capitals, and blank spaces to distinguish your page.

Companies > Simple Local Business (edit mode)

Overview   Products & Services   Follower Insights   Page Insights   Employee Insights

This page was last edited on 12/18/2012 by **Courtney Robertson**

Optimize your Company Name and Description for: [English ⬍]

* **Company Name**

Simple Local Business

* **Company Description**

Simple Local Business helps small and local business owners with their marketing, website development, productivity, and business operations. Members of this group are eager help each other brainstorm and form masterminds that empower each other to reach their full potential and best serve their communities.

Default Language: [English ⬍]

Members will see the Company Name and Description that matches their language preference. Otherwise, we will display your Default Language selection.

Include at least one trusted employee as an administrator if applicable. This person must also have the company domain as part of their email, be following the company page, and be connected to you personally.

Company Pages Admins

Designated Admins

You must be connected to a member to include them as an admin.

Start typing a name

Courtney Robertson   ☒
Digital Marketing Strategist, Public Speaker, Author, Owner, Trainer
at Simple Local Business

Next, you'll upload your logo and cover images in a few sizes:
- Cover art: 640 x 220px (not required to be your logo)
- Logo 100 x 60px
- Company square logo 50 x 50px
- Company comment logo 30 x 30px

Image

Edit

Standard Logo

Edit

Square Logo

Edit

Square logo is used in the network updates.

Next, add the specialties that your company offers. This could be areas of focus, specific services offered, or your most popular products. Your specialties can be up to 256 characters in length.

Company Specialties

social media training	website development
digital marketing	productivity
business procedures	computer training
speaking	social media policy development
WordPress	mobile marketing
email marketing	local seo
ecommerce	

⊕ Add more specialties

If your company administrates groups, this is the place to showcase these groups. You can feature only 3 groups in this area, even if your company has more groups than that.

Featured Groups

You must be either a member or an admin of each group to feature it on your company page.

Start typing the name of a group - You can add 2 more groups

Simple Local Business
2 members

Select the appropriate information on the Company types

*Company Type

Self Owned ⬍

*Company Size

myself only ⬍

*Company Website URL

http://simplelocalbusiness.com

*Main Company Industry

Professional Training ⬍

*Company Operating Status

Operating ⬍

Year Founded

2013

Finally, if you have more than one location, include these. Up to 5 locations are supported.

Company Locations
(Add up to 5 different locations)

Simple Local Business

Second Street
Chambersburg, PA 17201
United States

Edit

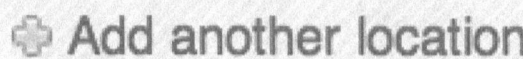 Add another location

Careers

If your company is a paying member of the LinkedIn Jobs feature, you can enable posting open jobs on the Careers tab.

Products & Services

You have the opportunity to feature up to 10 different products and services on your Products page. The header graphic should be 646 x 222px and you have 100 characters for the product title and up to 2,000 characters to describe your product, and you actually have formatting options like Bold, Italics, and Bullets. Note that you can include a Youtube video. This would be a great way to demonstrate the product in action. Your offers can be up to 500 characters to display as a preview on the right column of your products page.

Courtney Robertson

Overview **Products & Services** Follower Insights Page Insights Employee Insights

Publish Cancel

* Indicates required field

Step 1. Choose between a product or service

Would you like to add a product or service?*
- Product
- Service

Step 2. Select a category

Select a category that best fits your product/service

Choose category ▼ *

Step 3. Name your product or service

Product or Service name

Product name... *

Step 4. Add an image of your product or service.
Choose an image that represents your product or service. Your image will be re-sized to 100x80 pixels.

Image / Photo

100x80 pixels, .PNG, .JPG, or .GIF

✛ Add image

Step 5. Describe your product or service

Description *

B *I* U ☰ ☰
Write a brief description of the product...

Step 6. List of key features
Use this section to list the key benefits or use cases of your product or service.

Create a bulleted list of product/service features

✛ Add more features

Disclaimer

B *I* U ☰ ☰
Product Disclaimer

Step 7. Add a URL for this product or service
Use this section to link to a location on your website where LinkedIn members can learn more about this specific product or service.

Website

Enter a product or service URL...

Step 8. Add a contact from your company
If a LinkedIn member wants to contact your company or learn more about this product or service you can showcase who in your company they can contact. Start typing the name of the contact people in the boxes below. You must be connected to that member on LinkedIn to include them below.

Contact us

You can only add people that you are connected to on LinkedIn

Employee name...

Employee name...

Employee name...

Step 9. Add a promotion for this product or service
Do you have a promotion or special offer for this product or service? Include a title, description and URL where users can click to learn more.

Create a special promotion

Give it a title

Enter a URL

Write a brief description of the promotion...

Step 10. Add a YouTube video about this product or service
Do you have a YouTube video about this product or service? Add a title for your video here.

Title your video

Video Header

Step 11. Add your YouTube video URL.
Copy and paste the URL from your YouTube video in the box below.

YouTube Video URL

YouTube Video URL

LinkedIn also enables variations of your Products tab. You can have up to 3 rotating images at the top of the page and specify the order that various products display. Go to your Products tab and click Edit.

Courtney Robertson

Overview **Products** Follower Insights Page Insights Employee Insights

Publish   Cancel

Step 1. Create multiple variations of this page

You can create versions of this page to be served to custom audiences based on their profile content. For example, you can create a version targeted to people in the United States, and a different version targeted to members in Canada. Once you have created a "default" version, create different versions by clicking "New Audience" above. Name your target, choose your targeting characteristics and click "Save and Exit" to edit your targeted page.

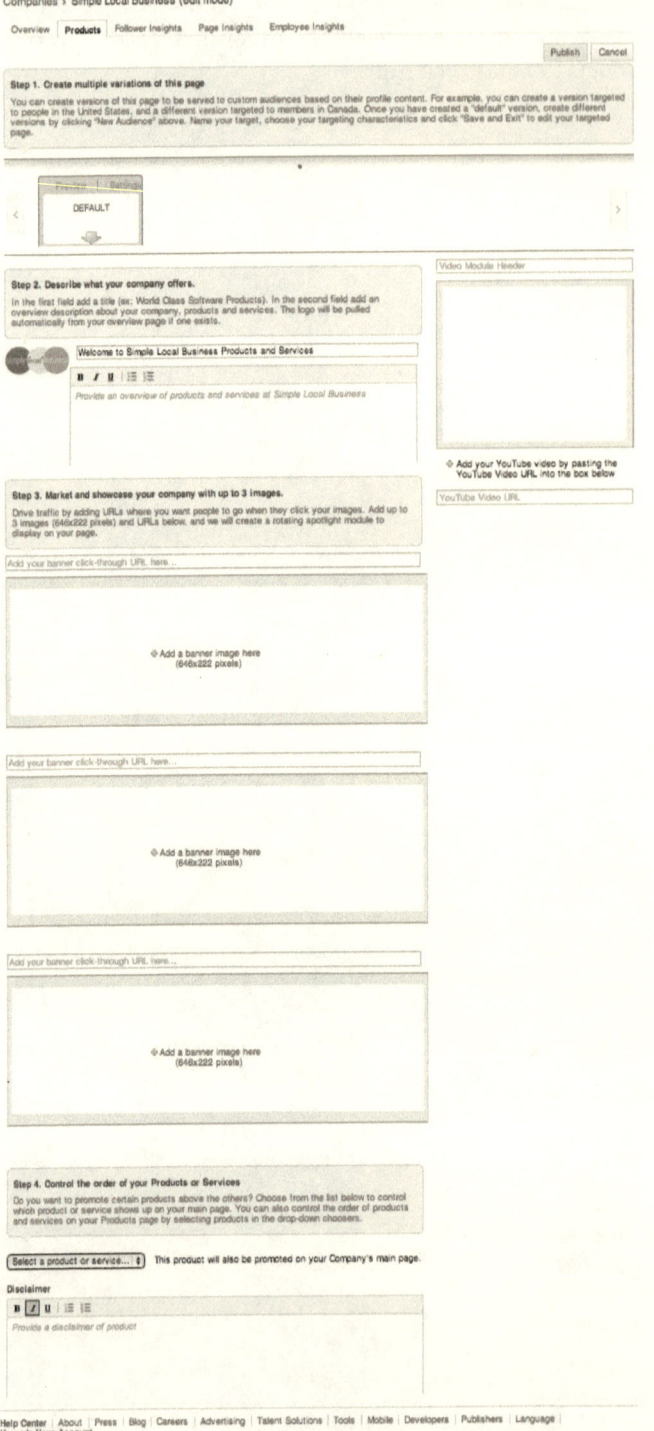

Step 2. Describe what your company offers.

In the first field add a title (ex: World Class Software Products). In the second field add an overview description about your company, products and services. The logo will be pulled automatically from your overview page if one exists.

Welcome to Simple Local Business Products and Services

B *I* **U** ≔ ≔

Provide an overview of products and services at Simple Local Business

Video Module Header

◇ Add your YouTube video by pasting the YouTube Video URL into the box below

YouTube Video URL

Step 3. Market and showcase your company with up to 3 images.

Drive traffic by adding URLs where you want people to go when they click your images. Add up to 3 images (646x222 pixels) and URLs below, and we will create a rotating spotlight module to display on your page.

Add your banner click-through URL here...

◇ Add a banner image here
(646x222 pixels)

Add your banner click-through URL here...

◇ Add a banner image here
(646x222 pixels)

Add your banner click-through URL here...

◇ Add a banner image here
(646x222 pixels)

Step 4. Control the order of your Products or Services

Do you want to promote certain products above the others? Choose from the list below to control which product or service shows up on your main page. You can also control the order of products and services on your Products page by selecting products in the drop-down choosers.

Select a product or service... ⬍   This product will also be promoted on your Company's main page.

Disclaimer

B *I* **U** ≔ ≔

Provide a disclaimer of product

After creating a default Products tab, again edit. Now you will be able to create a new audience segment, and narrow down the search results based upon who visits the page. You can specify various audiences see product offers specific to their niche. You can have up to 30 of these products pages.

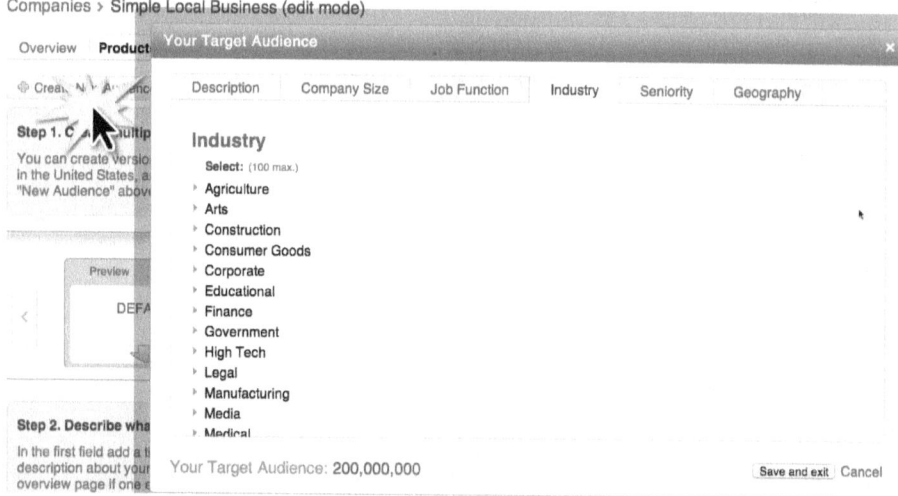

Once your products are published, you can request that your connections leave a review for a specific product. Do ask them for these reviews. Customize your own message and select customers most likely to leave you a positive review rather than spamming your entire network with requests.

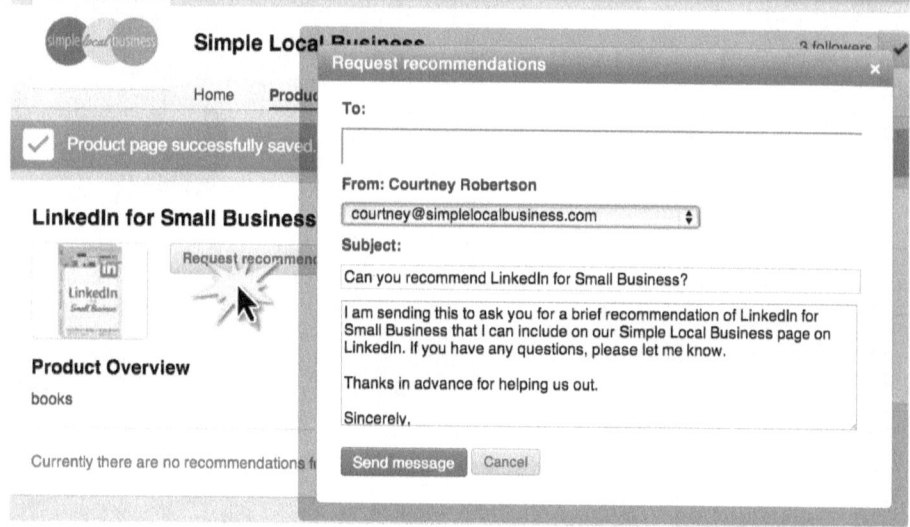

If your products are already published and viewable on the "Products" tab, you can also request a recommendation from there.

 **Simple Local Business**

Home **Products** Insights

 **LinkedIn for Small Business**

books

Request recommendations Share

On your own website you can also request reviews. The code for a recommend button on your site can be found at https://developer.linkedin.com/plugins/recommend-button

Build a Recommend Button

Enter a company name

company name...   (?)

Enter a product ID

product ID...   (?)

Choose a count mode

Vertical	Horizontal	No Count
4,216		
in Recommend	**in** Recommend ‹ 312	**in** Recommend

Get Code

Showcase Pages
If your brand has products with enough recognition of their own, a Showcase

<u>Page</u> could be useful. Announced in November 2013, these pages are much like a company page but focused around a brand within the parent company.

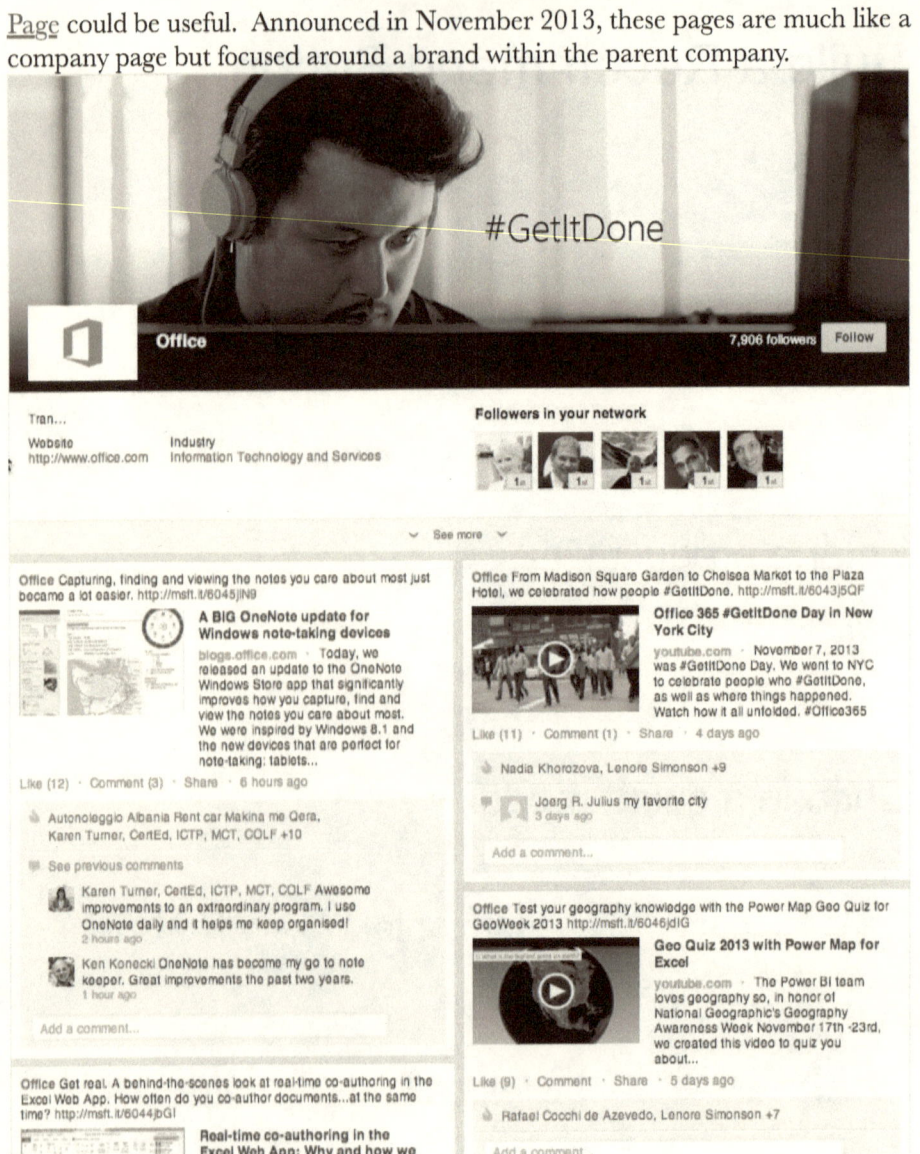

When browsing a company page that has showcase pages within, look for it to be displayed on the sidebar:

Other Microsoft pages

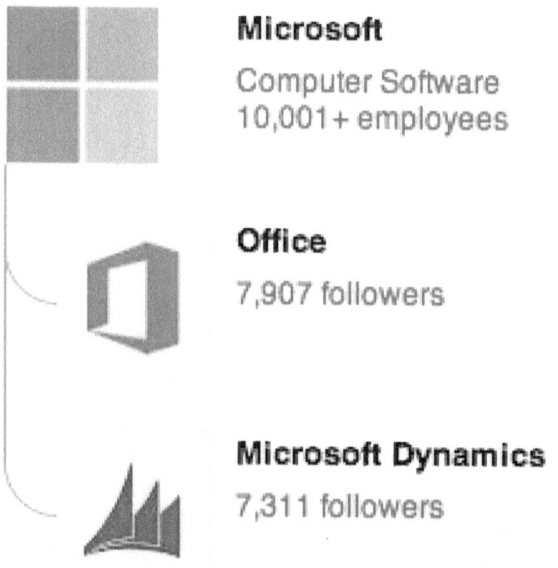

Microsoft

Computer Software
10,001+ employees

Office

7,907 followers

Microsoft Dynamics

7,311 followers

To create your showcase page, click the edit drop-down menu.

Fill in the information to finish setting up your page:

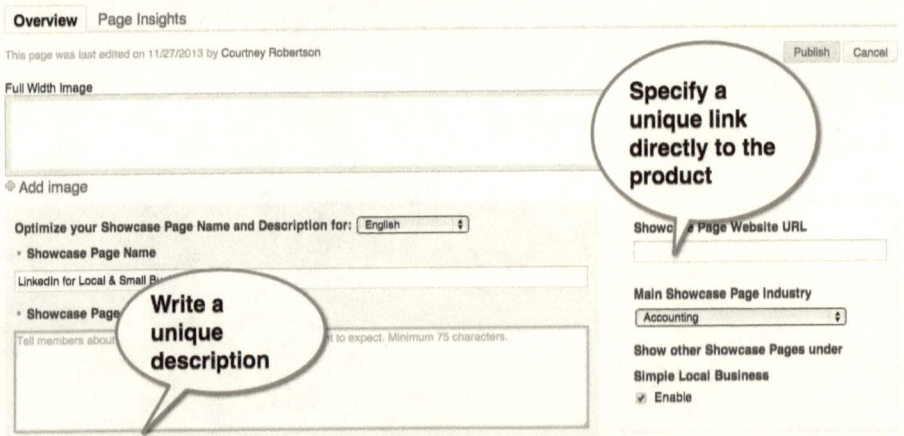

Notice that you will be able to manage page insights for the showcase pages.

This will lead to direct targeting for customers interested specifically in the unique product within the larger company.

Page Insights

While editing your page, notice that you can get a view of your page insights. These insights can include details about those following your page, those engaging with the content your page has provided, and if your company has employees listed, you'll discover insights on their LinkedIn activity.

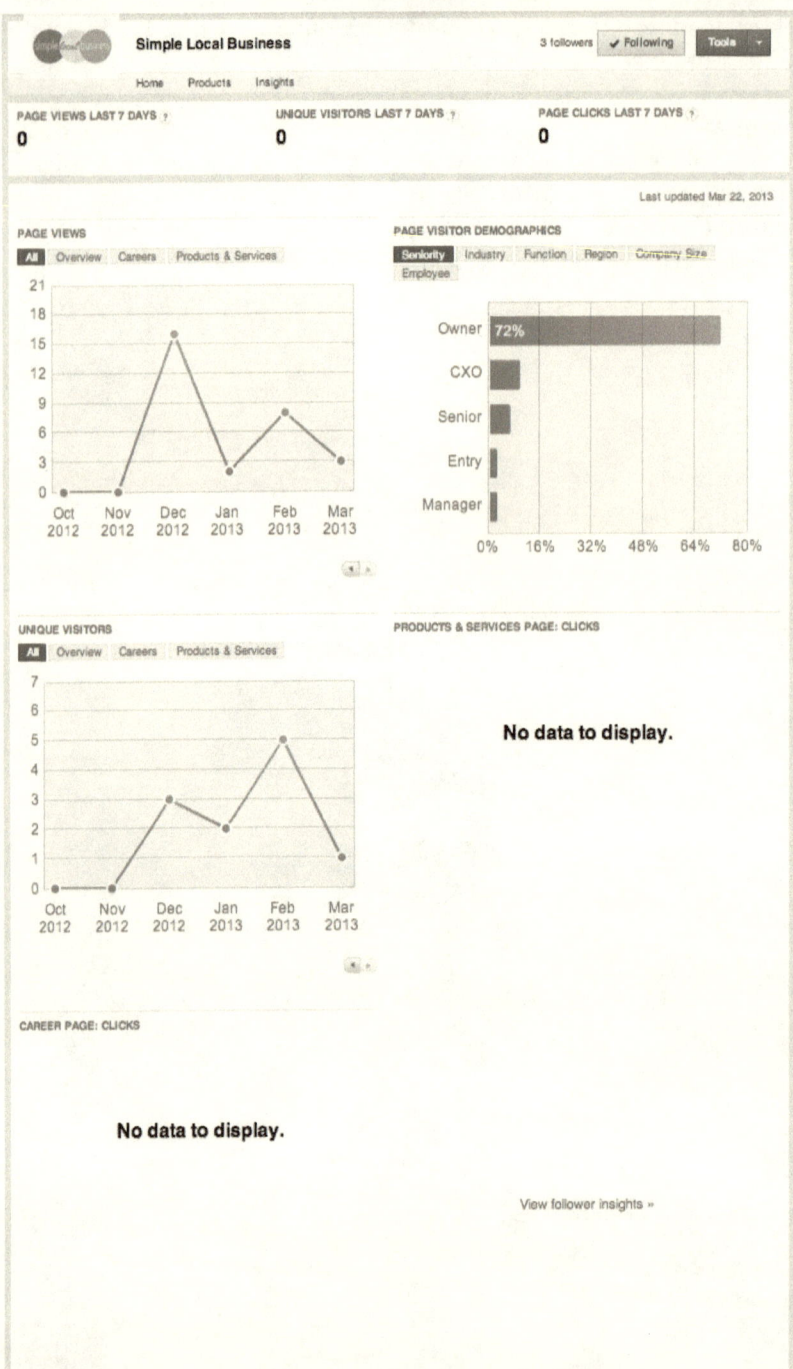

 **Simple Local Business**

3 followers ✓ Following Tools ▾

Home   Products   Insights

TOTAL FOLLOWERS ?	TOTAL IMPRESSIONS LAST 7 DAYS ?	NEW FOLLOWERS LAST 7 DAYS ?
3	**19** (+850.0%)	0
IMPRESSIONS/UPDATE LAST 7 DAYS ?	UPDATES LAST 7 DAYS ?	UPDATE ENGAGEMENT LAST 7 DAYS ?
0 (◆)	**31** (+19.2%)	N/A

Charts last updated Mar 22, 2013

COMPANY UPDATE ENGAGEMENT

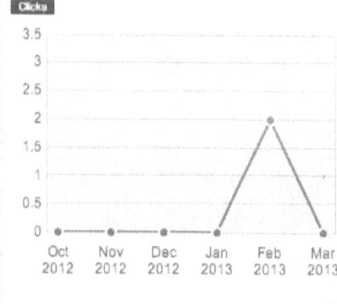

FOLLOWER DEMOGRAPHICS

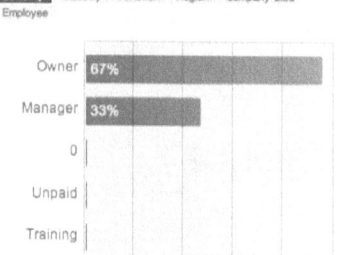

COMPANY UPDATE IMPRESSIONS

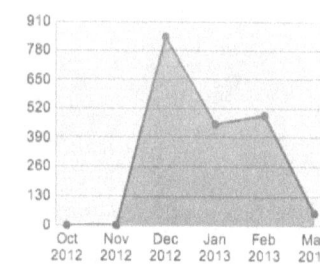

RECENT FOLLOWERS

Courtney Robertson [YOU]
Digital Marketing Strategist, Public Speaker, Author, Owner, Trainer at Simple Local Business
Harrisburg, Pennsylvania Area | Professional Training & Coaching

MEMBERS FOLLOWING

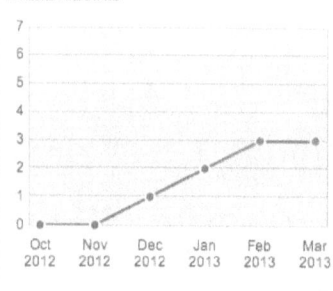

NEW FOLLOWERS

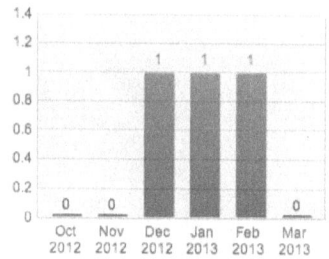

Using your Company Page Strategically

Once your company page is created, you will need to keep this page up-to-date. Each time that you have a new product or area of service, be sure to include that on your products page. On a daily basis, update your company status and reply to any comments. Monthly, take a look at your insights. Once you have 100 followers of your company page, you can send targeted status updates. Targets status updates enable your company to filter who can see a status update based upon several criteria: Inudstry, Seniority, Job Function, Company Size, Non-company Employees, and Geography.

Connecting your profile to your employer's company page

Be sure that your company is appropriately linked from your personal profile. Edit your experience in your profile.

 EXPERIENCE

Company Name *

Simple Local Business Change Company | Edit Display Name

Display Name

Simple Local Business

Then view your profile (not in edit mode) to be sure that your company logo displays.

 EXPERIENCE

Digital Marketing Strate ✦ **Public Speaker, Author, Owner, Trainer**
Find others with this title
Simple Local Business
February 2012 – Present (1 year 2 months) | Chambersburg, PA

For Your Website

Once your page is created, you can promote it on your website. LinkedIn offers a widget to place on your website and really is as easy as copy/paste.

Follow Button

If you'd like a simple "follow" button for visitors to follow your company page, you can add that at https://developer.linkedin.com/plugins#follow-company

Follow Company Plugin

Make it easy for prospective customers, job-seekers, and business partners to engage with your company.

Adding a Follow Company plugin to your website lets you quickly and easily grow your LinkedIn Company Page community so you can engage with your target audience, develop relationships, and acquire leads.

When a user clicks on the Follow Company button, they will automatically begin following your Company Page. Status updates you post from your Company Page will now show up on each follower's homepage. Encourage followers to like, share, and comment on your posts- this helps spread the word to your followers' entire network.

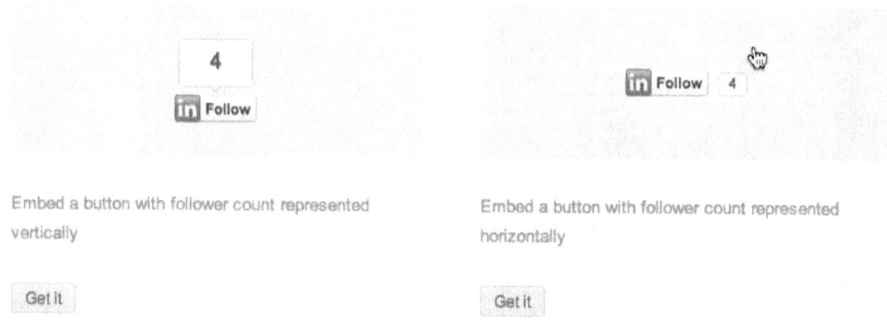

Embed a button with follower count represented vertically

Embed a button with follower count represented horizontally

Get it

Get it

If you'd like a slightly more detailed display, see the company profile widget at https://developer.linkedin.com/plugins#company-profile

Company Profile

Bring LinkedIn company profiles to your site to display key company information at-a-glance.

Make your site content richer by showing the summary, location, logo, and number of employees for companies featured on your site. Also, help users discover who they know at a company and enable them to track news and insights by using the follow button.

Get it

And consider using the more complete information on your company about page at https://developer.linkedin.com/plugins#insider

Company Insider

Enhance your content and show rich personalized insights about companies featured on your site.

Show users customized information, including who in their network works at a particular company, and the list of new hires and job changes at the company. Users can also follow a company with one click to track news and insights.

Get it

Company Recommendations

If you'd like to reviews for various products or services that your company offers, you can request recommendations on your site at https://developer.linkedin.com/plugins#recommend.

Recommend with LinkedIn

Enable users to recommend your products and services to LinkedIn's professional audience, and drive traffic back to your site.

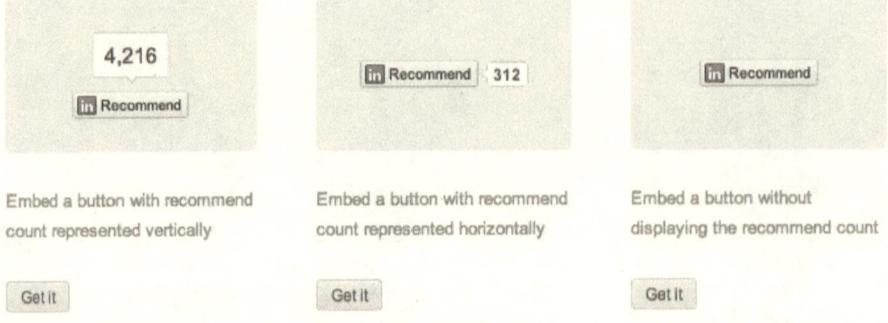

Embed a button with recommend count represented vertically

Get it

Embed a button with recommend count represented horizontally

Get it

Embed a button without displaying the recommend count

Get it

STUDENTS PREPARING FOR LIFE AFTER SCHOOL

LinkedIn has been known as a way for alumni to connect with each other, and even a place for college students nearing graduation to prepare their profiles before the job hunt. That is all changing with an announcement LinkedIn shared on August 19, 2013. LinkedIn is creating a special educational section including university pages, rather that merely alumni statistics and forcing universities to list as a company page.

In addition, high school students will soon be allowed in to create profiles. This exact age varies based upon country rules, but is approximately 14.

To view LinkedIn's educational focus, view http://linkedin.com/edu

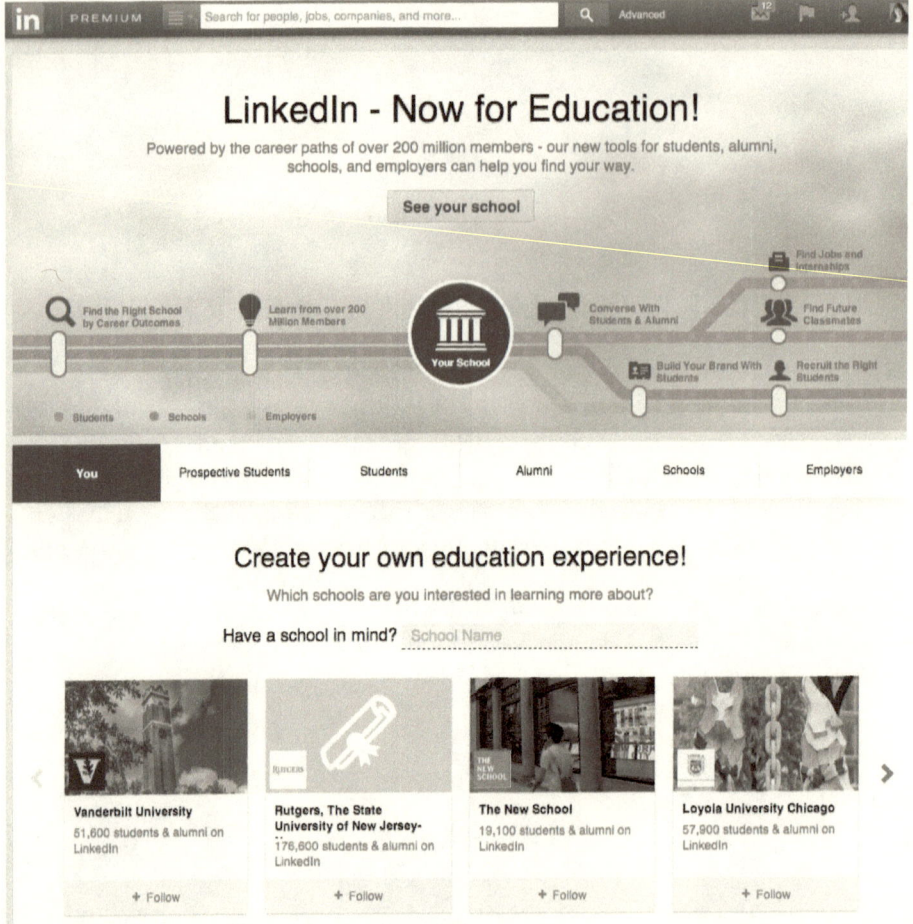

A big advantage to building your profile while still a full-time student is the ability on your profile to include classes, honors and awards, and a way to upload sample work. Additionally, you should request recommendations from teachers and professors that you have worked with at length, such as in your specific area of study or supervisors of extra-curricular activities.

It is also important to start networking now. Connect with your classmates, former managers, club presidents, and guest speakers. Get to know people in your industry while you have plenty of time before you start actively job seeking. Interact with these connections. This may lead to internships and job interviews.

When crafting your professional headline, consider something like: "Computer Science at Bloomsburg University | Captain of Swim Team | Aspiring Teacher | Student Ambassador".

While you may not have lots of work experience yet, the key is to just get started. Build your profile and come back to add content regularly.

Use LinkedIn to find possible companies that you would consider applying for.

Follow these companies now and watch what positions they have available. Find people holding the job positions that you want and connect with them if possible.

Also search for jobs now, even if you are years away from applying. Learn what the employers are seeking and what they are offering. Researching the job market while you have plenty of time to evaluate what is ideal for you will benefit you greatly when it is time to apply.

Connect with Your School:

LinkedIn has begun allowing universities to have pages that are not company pages. See if your school has created their page yet. If so, indicate that you are either a prospective student, enrolled, alumni, or staff. While here you can view statistics about alumni information, and details about the school.

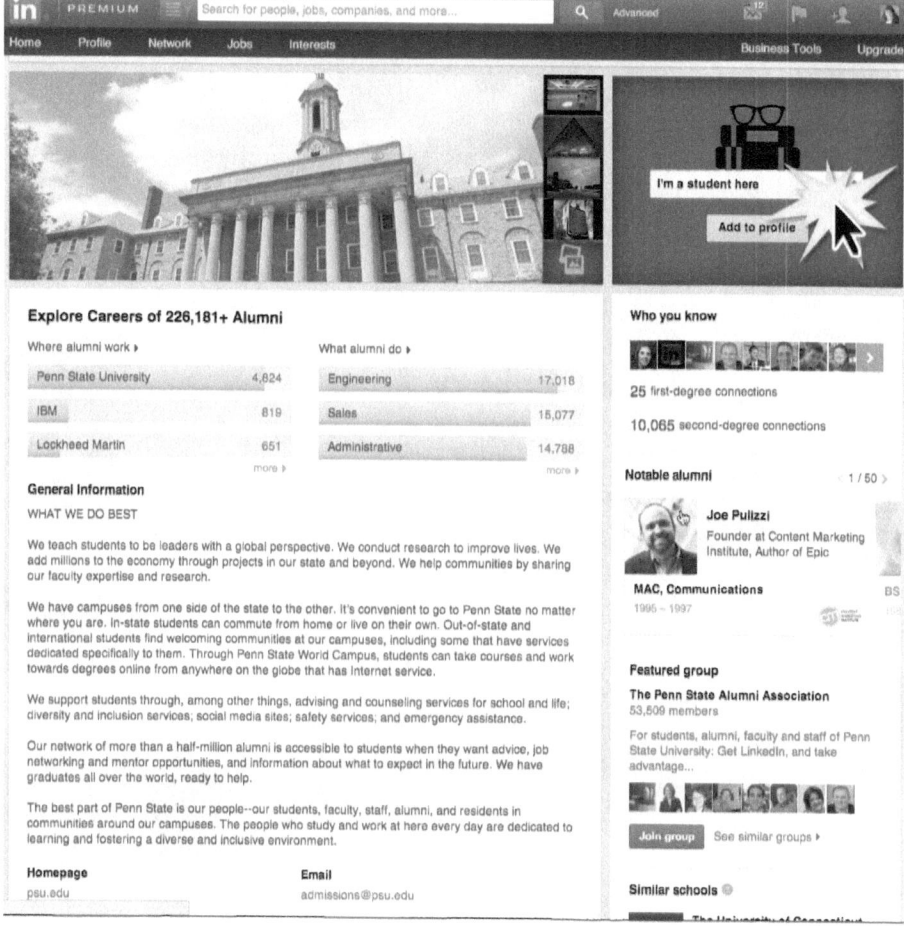

Notice who you may already know that has indicated they also are students or alumni. These are people that you should consider for recommendations.

Who you know

25 first-degree connections

10,065 second-degree connections

Notable alumni may be included as LinkedIn Influencers and hold positions of significance within larger corporations. Ideally when contacting these alumni mention the school, your interest in finding mentors and potential places for internships.

Notable alumni   ‹ 9 / 50 ›

While viewing the school page, you can find valuable connections to have. Whether you have graduated or not, you can join the alumni group.

Featured group

The Penn State Alumni Association
53,509 members

For students, alumni, faculty and staff of Penn State University: Get LinkedIn, and take advantage...

Join group   See similar groups ▶

If you are a student still considering where to attend school, the Similar Schools area may be of interest to you.

Similar schools

The University of Connecticut
United States

Lehigh University
United States

University of Illinois at Urbana-Champaign
United States

Rutgers, The State University of New Jersey-New Brunswick
United States

University of Delaware
United States

University of Pittsburgh
United States

"See also" pages are integrating the "Company page" that was created prior to university pages debut. If you have interest in a career as staff at the school, it may be interesting to follow the company page.

See also...

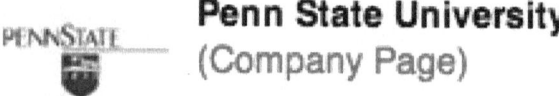

Penn State University
(Company Page)

NEWS

LinkedIn Today is customized news that displays in your main dashboard and can be customized or viewed individually. It is located at http://linkedin.com/today.

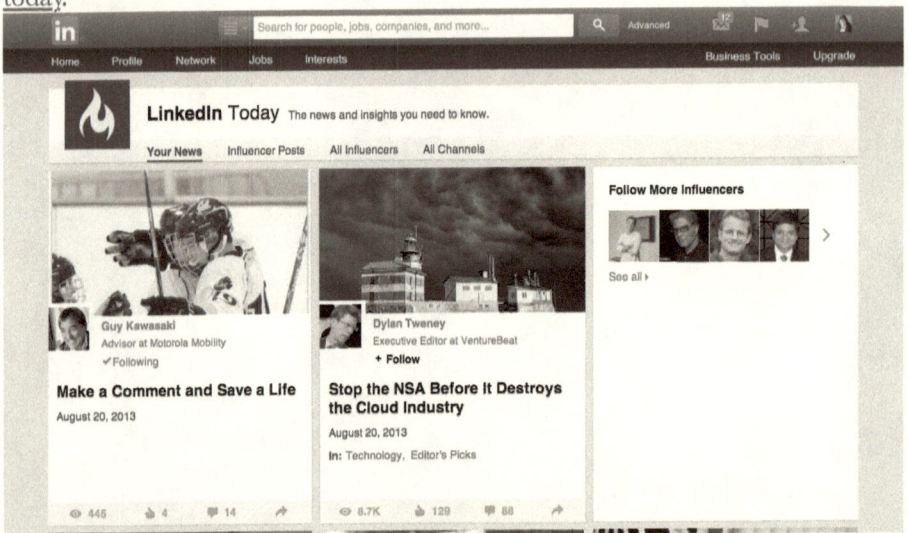

Select the content that you would like to view updates about by visiting All Influencers and All Channels. Find and follow what you'd like.

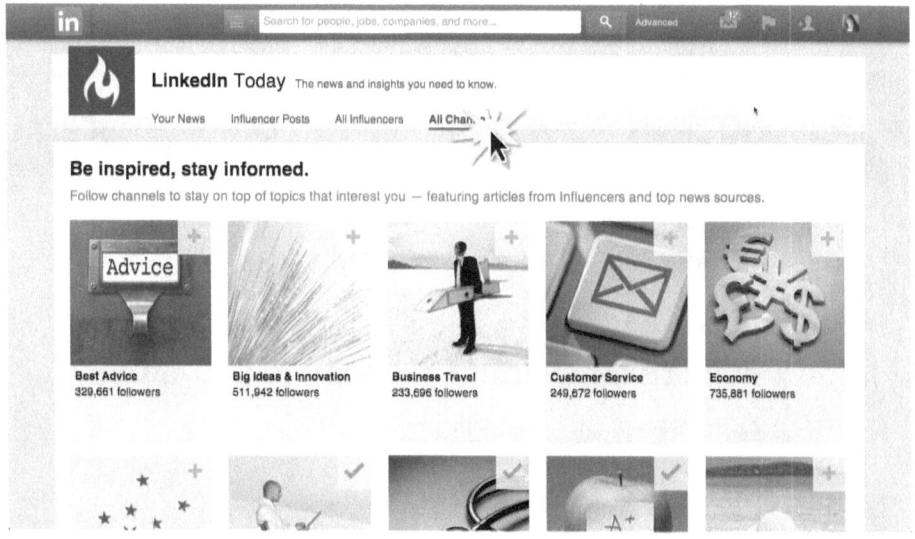

Remember that these articles will be seen in your main LinkedIn dashboard each time that you log in. Others will not see what you subscribe to.

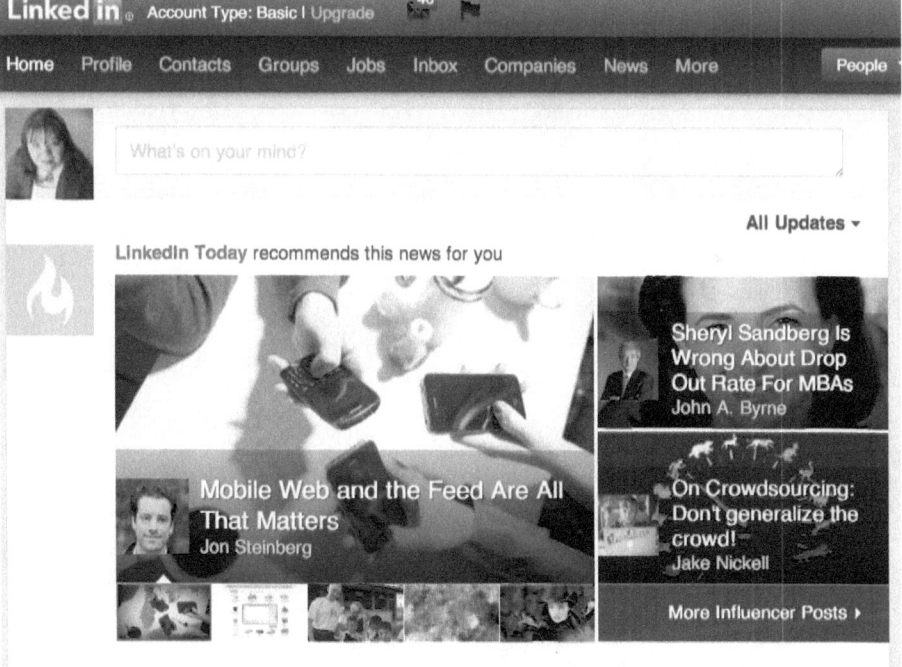

LinkedIn Today can be a great way to stay on top of news in your industry and find sources of content that you can share with your network. News from across the web and most shared by your connections will be displayed in the LinkedIn Today content along with the areas that are relative to your preferences.

You can read the articles inside LinkedIn and view the comments that others have left. You can also share it from here to other other networks.

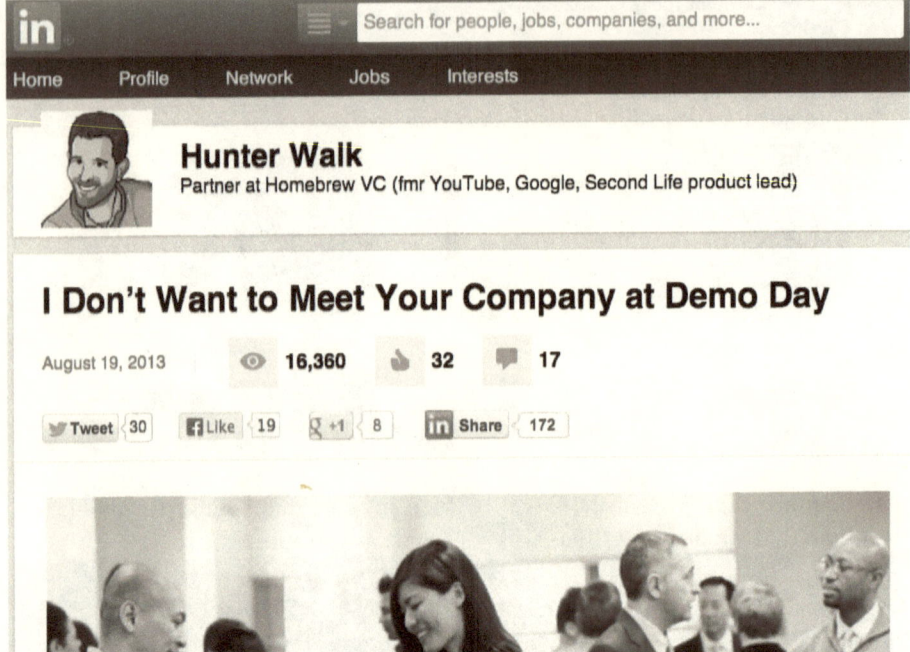

MOBILE APPS AND TOOLS

LinkedIn offers a variety of additional ways to extend your experience. Whether mobile apps, browser extensions, toolbars and signatures for your email, or other interesting ways to view your LinkedIn content, you can really expand your network and enjoy discovery on the go.

Mobile Apps

LinkedIn offers a mobile app to interact from your phone or tablet. The app is available on iOS, Android, Windows, and Blackberry. Depending what activity I am participating in, I sometimes prefer to use the mobile app over the computer. Groups tend to be a great experience from the mobile app. Within the app, you can access most all of the features that the computer browser has to offer, including viewing other's profiles. Consider connecting with others that you are networking with in person on LinkedIn at the networking event. It is a fast way to find each other while you are thinking about it.

Aside from the LinkedIn mobile app, LinkedIn provides a business card app, CardMunch. With it, you can scan another person's business card and save their contact information to your phone. When you load the LinkedIn app, you can grant it permission to scan your address book for contacts that may also be on LinkedIn. This is a powerful app when you are receiving and processing a large number of business cards.

LinkedIn Labs

LinkedIn Labs offers a variety of interesting tools, some of which help you visualize your network. Labs includes:

- Veterans and Mocha for assisting military personnel in finding employment after service
- Year-in-review, InMaps, and Connection Timeline to help you see how you have connected with others
- Resume Builder
- Swarm and Instant Search to share what others are searching for
- And more interesting fun finds

LinkedIn Tools

LinkedIn offers additional tools to help you extend your network.

- Share on your website to LinkedIn

- Slideshare - A repository for all your slidedeck presentations, LinkedIn acquired Slideshare and now integrates it nicely into personal profiles. Use it to upload your PowerPoint, Keynote, or other slide presentations and embed them into your own website.
- The Outlook Toolbar - allows you to see LinkedIn inside the MS Outlook software
- Email Signature - for sharing your LinkedIn profile with those you email
- Sharing BookMarklet - easily share any open webpage to a LinkedIn Status Update link
- Profile Badges - to place on your website encouraging visitors to connect with you

Third-party Tools

While not official tools, a few of these can really help you maximize your LinkedIn experience. Here are several that I like:

- Rapportive - added to your Gmail experience, you can see a preview of the sender's latest updates if you are connected, or request connecting if you haven't yet.
- Hootsuite - the best social media management dashboard. Not only does it work with all other social media networks, but with it you can manage your personal profile, groups, and company page updates, as well as replying to others.
- Buffer - for sharing an article or link at a slightly later time. Buffer will determine when it is best to publish the update.
- IFTTT - If This Then That - with this tool you can specify a wide array of actions, such as if you publish a blog post then share it as a LinkedIn status update automatically.
- JibberJobber - for job hunters, recruiters, and hiring professionals
- WordPress JetPack Publicize - if you use WordPress to run your own website, you can use this plugin to send any new blog posts to a LinkedIn Status Update Link automatically

ADS

LinkedIn, like most other social networks, allows advertisements in a variety of ways. The three main categories of advertisements are:
1. Ads
2. Sponsored Updates (company page status) - see the Company chapter for more information
3. Sponsored InMail - multimedia email messages delivered through the LinkedIn inbox, including videos.

To create an ad, start at http://linkedin.com/ads.

Sidebar Ads
The first means is by running ads on the sidebar of LinkedIn.

Grow Your Career by Following:
The Cosmopolitan of Las Vegas

Courtney Robertson

The Cosmopolitan of Las Vegas

Courtney, get the latest on The Cosmopolitan of Las Vegas Jobs, News & more!

Follow Company

This method has been available since LinkedIn launched nearly.

You will have a chance to target which people see your ad. This is highly customizable, and when you are new to running ads it may be beneficial to start with a very narrow audience. To get started, from the Ads dashboard, click "get started". When presented with the following options, select "create an ad".

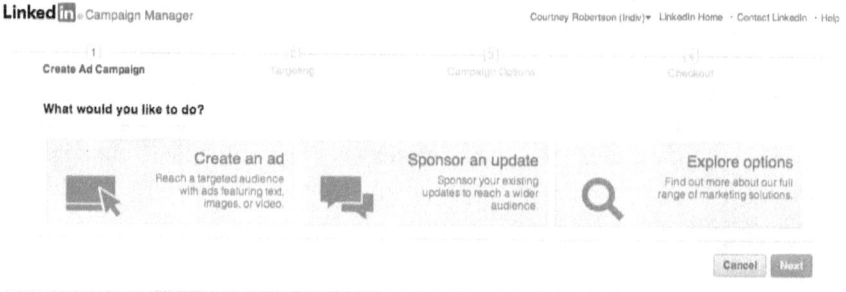

Targeting means to specify who should see this ad. The more you narrow this down to your ideal audience, the more effective your ads are likely to be. You won't need to spend money on ad displays for people outside your target audience. However, you will need to keep your audience broad enough to have at least 1,000 people in that audience.

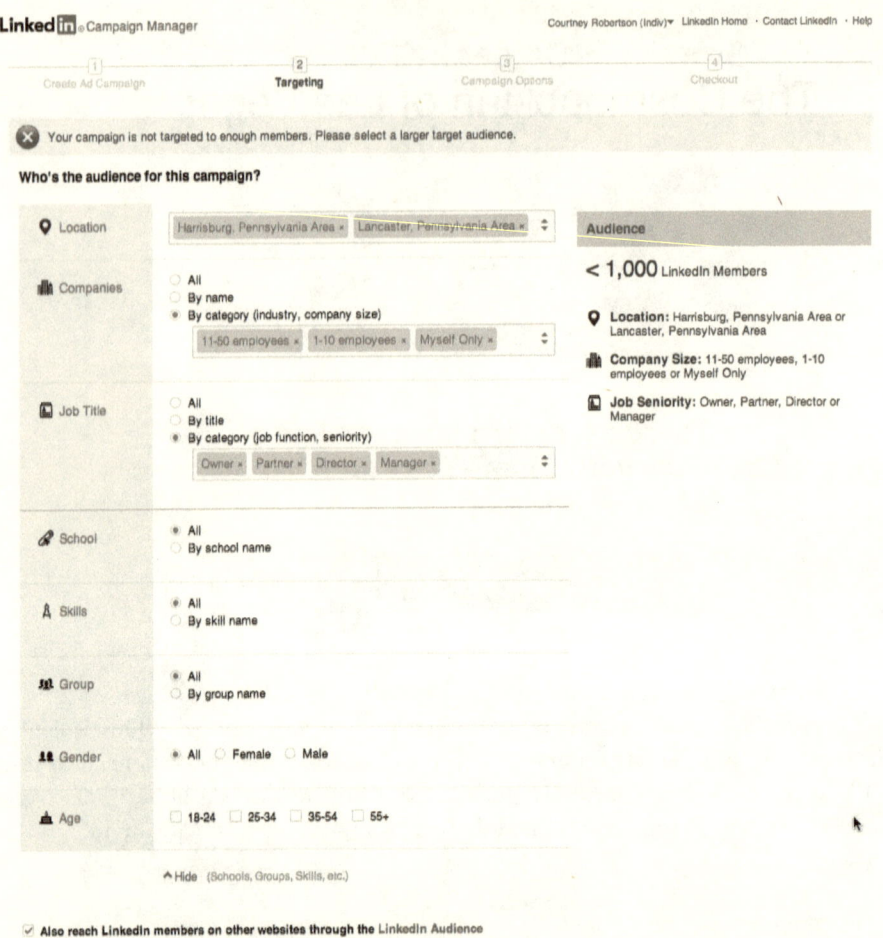

After drilling down into the exact audience members that should see the account, you then will have a chance set how much you are willing to spend. The higher you spend, the more likely you are to bump out others advertising to the same audience.

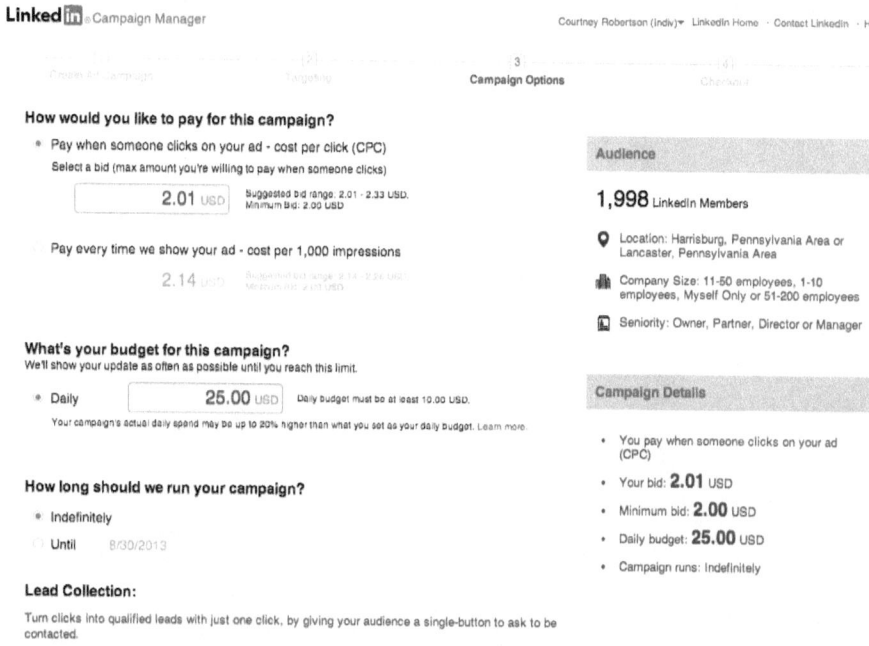

Create an campaign   Targeting   3 Campaign Options   4 Checkout

How would you like to pay for this campaign?

● Pay when someone clicks on your ad - cost per click (CPC)
Select a bid (max amount you're willing to pay when someone clicks)

| 2.01 USD | Suggested bid range: 2.01 - 2.33 USD. Minimum Bid: 2.00 USD |

Pay every time we show your ad - cost per 1,000 impressions

2.14 USD   Suggested bid range: 2.14 - 2.26 USD. Minimum bid: 2.03 USD

What's your budget for this campaign?
We'll show your update as often as possible until you reach this limit.

● Daily | 25.00 USD | Daily budget must be at least 10.00 USD.

Your campaign's actual daily spend may be up to 20% higher than what you set as your daily budget. Learn more.

How long should we run your campaign?

● Indefinitely

○ Until   8/30/2013

Lead Collection:

Turn clicks into qualified leads with just one click, by giving your audience a single-button to ask to be contacted.

✓ Turn on Lead Collection for this campaign. Learn More

[Back]   [Cancel] [Save changes]

Audience

1,998 LinkedIn Members

⦿ Location: Harrisburg, Pennsylvania Area or Lancaster, Pennsylvania Area

🏢 Company Size: 11-50 employees, 1-10 employees, Myself Only or 51-200 employees

📇 Seniority: Owner, Partner, Director or Manager

Campaign Details

● You pay when someone clicks on your ad (CPC)

● Your bid: **2.01** USD

● Minimum bid: **2.00** USD

● Daily budget: **25.00** USD

● Campaign runs: Indefinitely

And finally before your ad launches, complete your billing information:

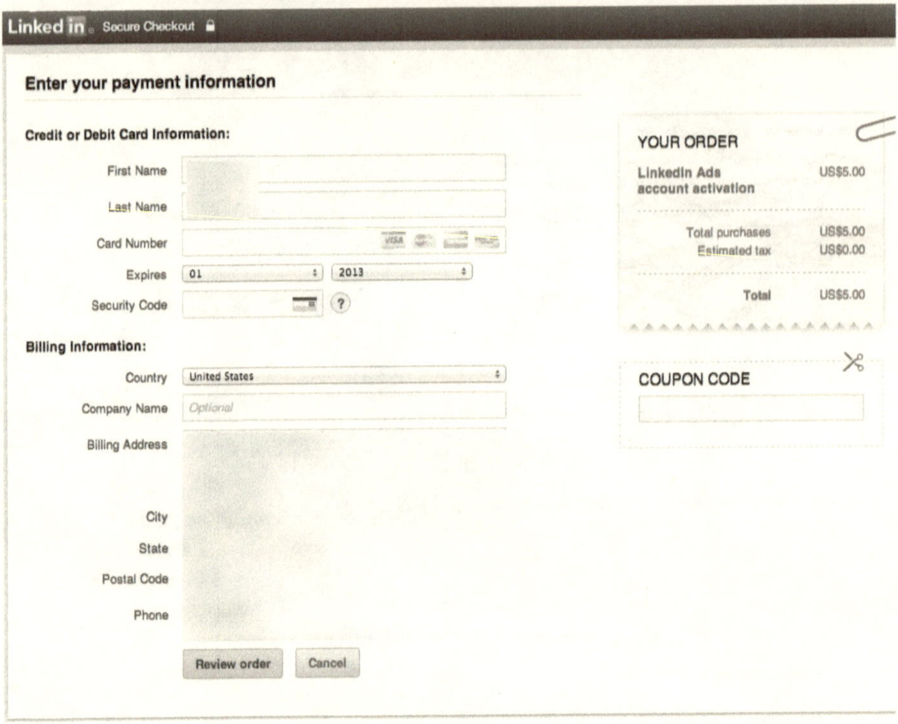

Linked in ® Secure Checkout 🔒

Enter your payment information

Credit or Debit Card Information:

First Name	
Last Name	
Card Number	VISA
Expires	01 ⬍ 2013 ⬍
Security Code	🔲 ?

Billing Information:

Country	United States ⬍
Company Name	*Optional*
Billing Address	
City	
State	
Postal Code	
Phone	

[Review order] [Cancel]

YOUR ORDER

LinkedIn Ads account activation	US$5.00
Total purchases	US$5.00
Estimated tax	US$0.00
Total	**US$5.00**

COUPON CODE ✂

Once your ad is running, you can go to https://www.linkedin.com/ads/home to manage your ads. This will show you the statistics of how your ads is performing, as well as creating a business account. A LinkedIn Ads Business Account is designed for companies that may have multiple people managing the ads and using company billing information.

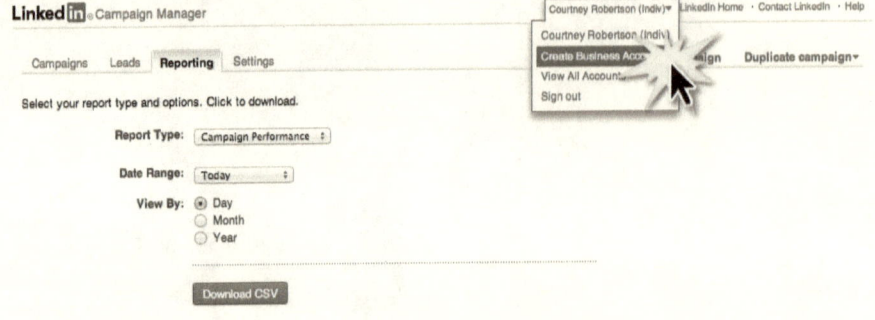

AVOID THESE COMMON MISTAKES

1. Unprofessional or poor quality profile photo. Your profile photo is often the first impression people have of you. If your photo is blurry, unprofessional, too yellow, or just not well lit, you've already given a less than stellar first impression. Whether you hire a photographer or just get a friend with decent photography skills to take your photo doesn't matter. Just get a quality headshot that you can use across your social media profiles.

2. Incomplete profile by LinkedIn's standards. LinkedIn will guide you through finishing your profile. Aim for at least 95% done. That last 5% will happen when you have employment and recommendations on your profile. Having it 95% done will give you an advantage in being discovered in search results.

3. Incomplete profile by my standards or lack of formatting. See the earlier chapter on completing your profile. Make your Summary pop by using bullets, and short, descriptive, keyword-rich phrases. Complete your specialties as well.

4. Neglecting your profile after finding employment. While you may no longer be seeking employment, learning how to network and refer business to others is a lifelong skill. It creates value in your professional network that may bring business or other opportunities back to you in the future. Continue to build your connections, and include media (like Youtube and Slideshare) of professional presentations and recognition.

5. Treating LinkedIn exclusively as a job board. LinkedIn may help you get a job, but you will want to think long term on your account here. Build your profile up extensively and grow your network. You may find that you become more valuable to your employer and thus receive a promotion. Likewise, you may find a better opportunity elsewhere and having your profile current and actively updated will help you stand out and be prepared for whatever comes.

6. Not connecting with professional people you meet. Any time you attend a networking event, conference, or even internal company meeting you have a chance to meet new people. Find them on LinkedIn, especially if

you have their business card in hand. Build that relationship in an ongoing way.

7. Missing customized profile URL. Using the default LinkedIn URL to your profile is a sure sign that you haven't finished your profile. With a unique link to your profile, such as http://linkedin.com/in/yourname, to use in your email signatures, you are sure to stand out.

8. Specialties and Skills not included. Being short on your specialties and skills is on par with being too lazy to finish out your profile. It may be uncomfortable to brag about your strengths, but it is needed here. These are the places that will help you turn up in search results.

9. Lacking media to support experience and education. You have a chance to demonstrate your professional skills by showcasing what you've done. If you've created a slide presentation, upload it to Slideshare and then link it to your job. Use services like Animoto to turn a photo set into a Youtube video.

10. Websites not customized. Rather than your profile saying "My Blog" or "Company Website" - rename these links to be the actual domain name.

11. Headline doesn't attract attention. Your headline should be a benefit statement that attracts others to view your profile. If it merely is your job title at your company, go change it now.

12. Career doesn't link to company page. If your company has a LinkedIn page, be sure that your employment clicks through to that company page.

13. No group memberships. If you aren't connected to a few valuable groups, you aren't as visible in search results. Connect to a few large groups simply to be discovered, and a few other groups that reflect your professional career or alumni affiliation.

14. Typos

15. Buzzwords - Overusing these words will limit your discoverability according to LinkedIn. Many others are also using these so find a few new words:

- Creative
- Organizational
- Effective
- Motivated
- Extensive experience
- Track record
- Innovative
- Responsible
- Analytical
- Problem solving

BACKING UP YOUR ACCOUNT

Once you've done all the hard work of creating your profile, you will want to take every precaution to back up all your data. This is hopefully just a precautionary measure, but it is hard to tell if LinkedIn may lock your account unexpectedly.

Exporting Your Profile

To back up your profile, export it as a PDF. This will allow you to open a version of your profile using Adobe Acrobat Reader or Google Chrome browser.

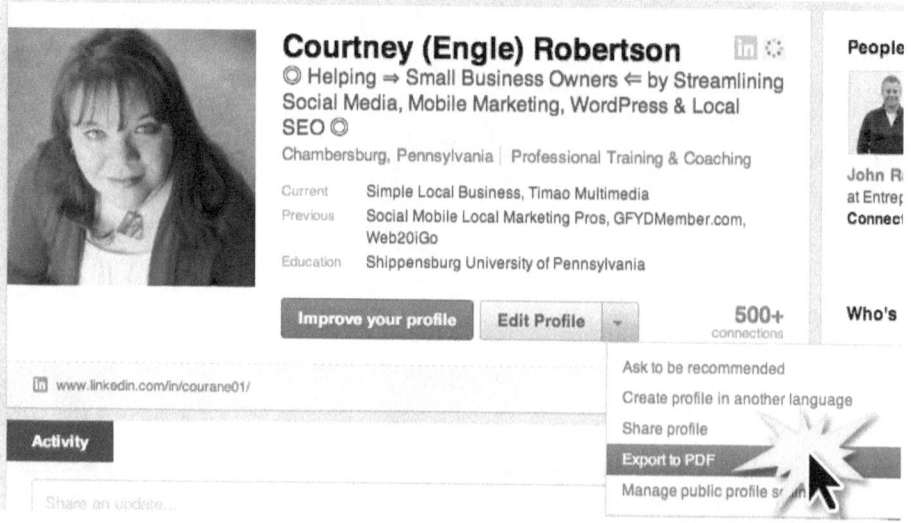

Exporting Your Connections

To export your connections, go to Network, Contacts, Settings or https://www.linkedin.com/contacts/manage_sources/ and select export contacts.

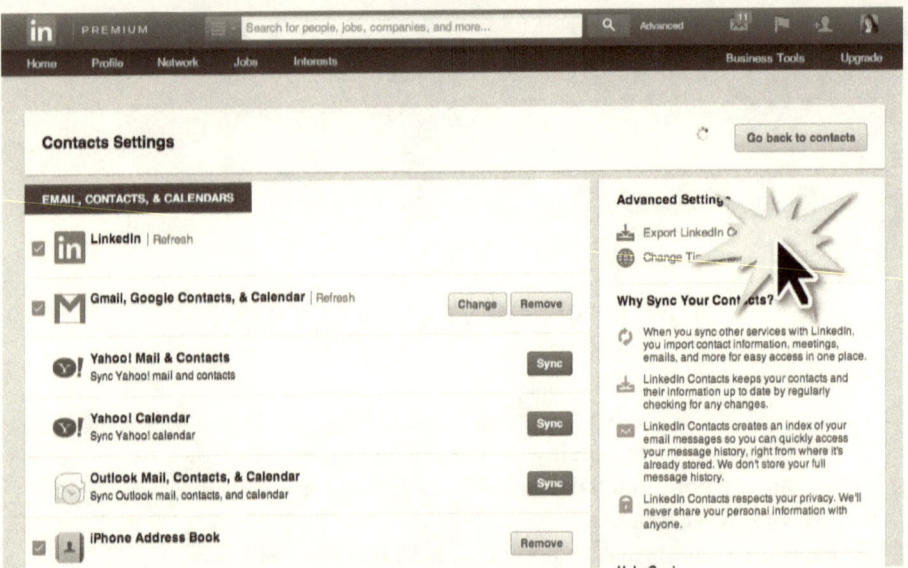

This will prompt you to download a ".csv" file format which can be easily imported into any email program or viewed as a spreadsheet in Excel, Numbers, or Google Drive.

LINKEDIN GLOSSARY

Connections - people that you are connected to on LinkedIn. These are made when others accept your invitation to connect or you accept someone else's invitation.

- **1st Degree Connections** - you are directly connected via an invitation to another LinkedIn member
- **2nd Degree Connections** - one of your 1st degree connections is connected to this member
- **3rd Degree Connections** - one of your 2nd degree connections is connected to this member

Invitation - a request to become first degree connections that you can send or receive

Your Network - all those that you have connected with, including 2nd or 3rd degree connections, and group members

Out of Network - a person that no one in your network or groups is connected to

Introductions - when you want to connect to a person that is not a 1st degree connection, you can request an introduction. This is a mutual email between the person you know, the person you want to meet, and yourself.

Public Profile - what anyone can see of your profile, whether they are logged in to LinkedIn or not.

Recommendations - References that coworkers and clients can provide about their experience working with you that appear publicly on your profile

Skills & Endorsements - Categories of services that you can perform that any connections can vouch for, whether they have ever experienced working with you or not.

Groups - organizations that members can join reflecting their professional, alumni, or interest affiliations

- **Open Group** - a group that anyone can join
- **Closed Group** - a group that is restricted to those invited exclusively or takes an application to join
- **Discussions** - much like a status update, often a question or a link shared

168

- **Promotions** - when members have something that solely benefits themselves or their company to share
- **Jobs** - group members may post jobs within groups for other members to see
- **Search**
- **Members** - view other group members
- **Group Rules** - review these before participating so as not to offend other members or get blocked from the group
- **Owner** - the creator of the group
- **Moderator** - limited administrative privileges to approve members, ban members, or flag suspicious content
- **Group Profile** - an overview of the group information
- **Group Statistics** - an overview of group members information

Update Feed - on the home page this displays all the updates of everyone in your network

Messages - an email inbox within LinkedIn to use with other members

InMail - private messages available to paying members or purchased to allow those who aren't connected to message each other.

Headline - a preview of your profile that displays your benefit statement or one sentence biography of your job description. This is prominently displayed when you post on groups, share an update, or reply to others.

Update - a status update that may contain a link or just text and is viewable by your network

Settings - privacy and notifications can be controlled in your settings. It is very important to review this before altering your profile.

Company Page - similar to profile pages, but for a company. These can feature products and services that the company offers as well as updates about job openings and discovering employees of that company. Members can follow companies, but must have an email from the companies domain to indicate that they are an employee.

LinkedIn Today - news from influencers and channels that can be viewed on http://linkedin.com/today or in the top of the update feed.

Influencer - people LinkedIn has partnered with to appear in the LinkedIn Today area that are thought or industry leaders

Channel - topics LinkedIn has curated related to various industries that appears in the LinkedIn Today area

OpenLink Network - paying or premium members of LinkedIn can network with each other without being connected

LION - a member adopted term for LinkedIn Open Networker. This is someone that practices connecting with most anyone that requests to connect

BONUS CONTENT

If you'd like to receive updates to this book as LinkedIn changes or additional bonus content, please sign up at http://simplelocalbusiness.com/books/linkedin/updates/.

If this book has helped you get started or further understand LinkedIn, please leave a review at http://simplelocalbusiness.com/books/linkedin/review-linkedin-local-small-business/